JOAN ELLIOTT

CROSS STITCH
Sentiments and Sayings

David & Charles

**To my niece Christina – may your creativity
always take you to a happy place.
With love from Aunt Joan**

A DAVID & CHARLES BOOK

First published in the UK in 2004
Designs, text and decorative artwork Copyright © Joan Elliott 2004
Photography and layout Copyright © David & Charles 2004

Distributed in North America
by F&W Publications, Inc.
4700 East Galbraith Road
Cincinnati, OH 45236
1–800–289–0963

A catalogue record for this book is available from the British Library.
ISBN 0 7153 1598 6

EXECUTIVE COMMISSIONING EDITOR • Cheryl Brown
EXECUTIVE ART EDITOR • Ali Myer
BOOK DESIGNER • Casebourne Rose Design Associates
PROJECT EDITOR AND CHART PREPARATION • Lin Clements
PHOTOGRAPHY • Lucy Mason

Printed in Italy by STIGE
for David & Charles
Brunel House   Newton Abbot   Devon

Visit our website at www.davidandcharles.co.uk

David & Charles books are available from all good bookshops; alternatively you can contact our
Orderline on (0)1626 334555 or write to us at FREEPOST EX2110, David & Charles Direct,
Newton Abbot TQ12 4ZZ (No stamp required UK mainland).

Contents

Introduction 4

Friendship 6

Welcome Baby .14

Sound Advice 20

Celtic Spirit 28

Home is Where Your Honey Is 36

In the Garden .40

Help Wanted .46

Wisdom of the East 52

Sweet Sentiments 60

All in a Day's Work 66

Wedding Wishes 72

Pure Indulgence 78

Heart Strings .86

Native American Wisdom 92

Charted Alphabets 98

Materials, Techniques and Making Up 99

DMC/Anchor Thread Conversions 102

Suppliers and Acknowledgments 103

About the Author 103

Index 104

Introduction

The earliest known signed and dated sampler was created over four hundred years ago. Samplers were once kept as needlework notebooks and passed from hand to hand. Stitchers would compile samples of patterns and techniques and use them for reference when embroidering clothing and household objects. Working on narrow pieces of costly linen in what was called counted thread work, these early band samplers displayed the skill and creativity of the individual needleworker. By the 17th century it became common practice for children to keep their own record of motifs, often incorporating their name and the date the sampler was finished.

Young schoolgirls would often stitch alphabets and numbers to show off their first attempts at their newly learned skills. Fruit baskets, hearts, flower-pots and simple figures were chosen to adorn early samplers, each added pattern a testimony to the stitcher's mastery of this gentle craft. Soon elaborate verses were added in addition to the alphabets.

By the late 18th and early 19th centuries the cross stitch became so popular in the working of samplers that it became known as the 'sampler stitch'. No longer popular as a reference piece, Victorian women presented their ornate 'Fancy Work' as gifts or proudly displayed their finished embroideries in their homes. The once functional sampler was becoming a highly decorative leisurely pastime.

Today we may stitch to give, to keep, or to make memories, but mostly just for the love of stitching.

I've designed this collection of sentiments and sayings to celebrate our lives – from the everyday routines of home and office to all the wonderful moments we wish to remember in a special way. There are gentle reminders for everyone in the house to lend a helping hand. When work is piled high on your desk and your patience seems at breaking point, post a notice to remind yourself that it is all in a day's work. Yield to sweet temptation with pure indulgences and spread words of love that tickle your heartstrings.

You can share the sweetest sentiments and good wishes with your loved ones by stitching up any one of the many cards, including ones for baby, parents and your closest friends. A garden sampler carries the beauty of the garden indoors and two loving teddy bears let us know the true meaning of home. There are designs to celebrate the pleasure of afternoon tea with friends, the joyous arrival of a baby and the tender vows of marriage. The ethereal beauty of the Orient, the spiritual grace of Native American culture and a benevolent Irish blessing offer cherished words of inspiration for everyone.

There are many ways to pass on these words of wisdom. Throughout the book you will find projects for sweet-scented sachets, lovely felt hangings, decorative plant pokes, a charming bowl lid and bookmark, and even a set of mindful fridge magnets. Choose your favourite projects and let their sentiments and sayings inspire your day and brighten your heart.

Happy stitching everyone!

Friendship

There is a special place in the heart for the ways in which true friendship evolves. The delicate lace-lined shelves, antique teapots and tiny rosebud border of this sampler bring to mind a lazy afternoon spent with a friend over a pot of freshly steeped tea. Confidences and joys are shared, trials and difficulties eased and the bond between two people grows and blossoms.

Two smaller designs have been inspired by the sampler: stitch them up as small greetings cards and share them with those friends that make your life special. Use these same designs to create a set of handy coasters to give as a hostess gift or to use when guests arrive.

Friendship Sampler

Stitch count
185h x 145w

Design size
33.5 x 26.5cm (13¼ x 10⅜in)

Materials

46 x 40cm (18¼ x 15½in) antique white 14-count Aida

DMC stranded cotton (floss) as listed in chart key

Tapestry needle size 24

1 Prepare for work, referring to Techniques if necessary. Find and mark the centre of the fabric and circle the centre of the chart (pages 10–13) with a pen. Use an embroidery frame if you wish.

2 Start stitching from the centre of the chart and fabric, using two strands of stranded cotton (floss) for cross stitches. Following the chart for colour changes, work all backstitches using one strand and work the French knots using two strands wrapped once around the needle.

3 Once all stitching is complete, check for missed stitches and then finish your picture by mounting and framing (see page 101).

Friendship Cards

Stitch count (each card)
41h x 41w

Design size (each card)
6 x 6cm (2¼ x 2¼in)

Materials
(for each card)

18.5 x 18.5cm (7¼ x 7¼in)
antique white 18-count Aida

DMC stranded cotton (floss)
as listed in chart key

Tapestry needle size 24

Suitable card mount

1 Prepare for work, referring to Techniques if necessary. Find and mark the centre of the Aida fabric and circle the centre of the chart with a pen.

2 Start stitching from the centre of the chart and fabric, using two strands of stranded cotton (floss) for the cross stitches. Following the chart for colour changes, work all French knots using two strands wrapped once around the needle and work all backstitches using one strand.

3 Once all stitching is complete, mount your embroidery in a suitable card (see page 101 and also suggestions for decorating cards).

Friendship Coasters

Stitch count (each coaster)
41h x 41w

Design size (each coaster)
7.5 x 7.5cm (3 x 3in)

Materials
(for each coaster)

21.5 x 21.5cm (8½ x 8½in)
Fiddler's Light 14-count Aida
(Charles Craft)

DMC stranded cotton (floss)
as listed in chart key

Tapestry needle size 24

7.5cm (3in) diameter Lucite
(plastic) coaster (available in
most needlework and craft shops)

1 Prepare for work, referring to Techniques if necessary. Find and mark the centre of the fabric and circle the centre of the chart with a pen. Use an embroidery frame if you wish.

2 Start stitching from the centre of the chart and fabric, using two strands of stranded cotton (floss) for cross stitches. Following the chart for colour changes, work all French knots using two strands wrapped once around the needle and work all backstitches using one strand.

3 Once all stitching is complete, mount your embroidery in a coaster according to the manufacturer's instructions.

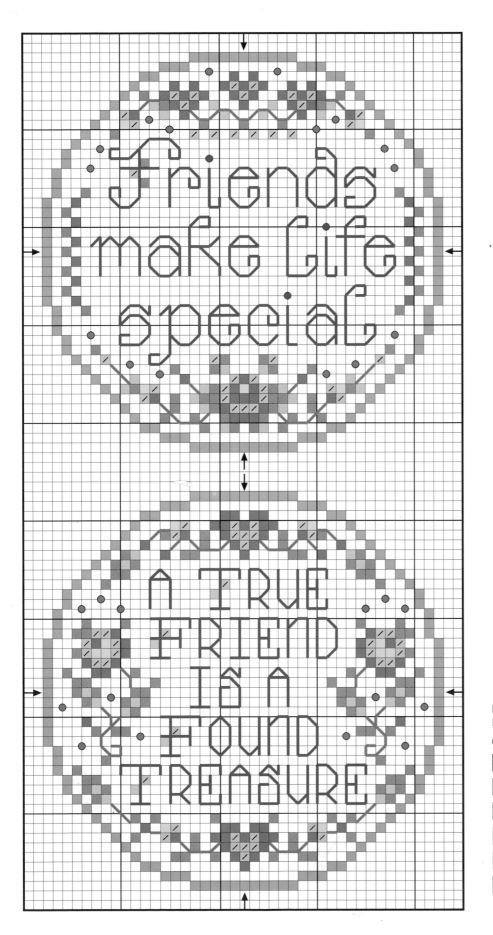

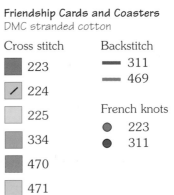

Friendship Cards and Coasters
DMC stranded cotton

Cross stitch		Backstitch	
■	223	—	311
╱	224	—	469
░	225		
■	334	French knots	
■	470	●	223
░	471	●	311

Friendship Sampler

DMC stranded cotton

Cross stitch

◼ 223	✕ 322	471	3753	∨ 3852	
╱ 224	△ 334	– 762	◉ 3755	• blanc	
225	◉ 415	╲ 775	3821		
◣ 311	469	932	3822		
312	+ 470	⌐ 3325	3823		

Backstitch
— 311
— 312 words
— 469
— 470
— 3799

French knots
● 312

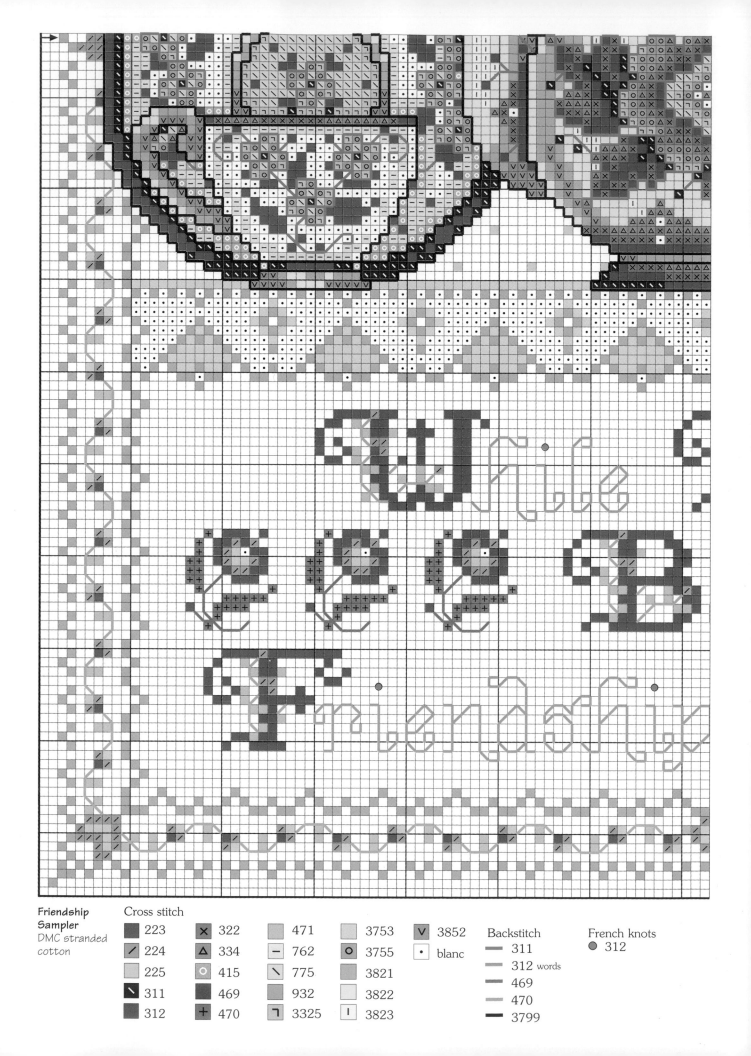

Friendship Sampler

DMC stranded cotton

Cross stitch

▨ 223	✖ 322	▨ 471	▨ 3753	⊽ 3852		
╱ 224	△ 334	– 762	◎ 3755	• blanc		
▨ 225	◎ 415	◥ 775	▨ 3821			
◣ 311	▨ 469	◥ 932	▨ 3822			
▨ 312	✚ 470	◰ 3325	▨ 3823			

Backstitch
— 311
— 312 words
— 469
— 470
— 3799

French knots
● 312

Welcome Baby

Fluffy bunnies, a calico cat, teddies galore, even a purple elephant – a child's world is a magical place. An assortment of cuddly creatures in soft colours drift down amongst the stars while guardian angels shower blessings upon them. Welcome your precious little one and create a lasting personalized record with baby's name and birth date on this enchanting birth announcement.

Two gift cards, suitable for framing, are included in this chapter. They are quick and easy to stitch up and either would make a wonderful addition when presenting the sampler to the proud parents. Two teddies celebrate the joy of the birth of twins and one new arrival rests on a fluffy cloud under the stars.

Welcome Baby Sampler

Stitch count
155h x 116w

Design size
28 x 21cm (11⅛ x 8¼in)

Materials
40.5 x 33.5cm (16 x 13¼in) antique white 14-count Aida

DMC stranded cotton (floss) as listed in chart key

Tapestry needle size 24

1 Prepare for work, referring to Techniques if necessary. Find and mark the centre of the fabric and circle the centre of the chart (pages 18–19) with a pen. Use an embroidery frame if you wish.

2 Start stitching from the centre of the chart and fabric. Work over one block of Aida, using two strands of stranded cotton (floss) for full cross stitches and three-quarter cross stitches. Following the chart for colour changes, work all French knots using two strands wrapped once around the needle and work all backstitches using one strand. Use the alphabet charted on page 98 to stitch the names and dates of your choice. Plan the letters and numbers on graph paper first to ensure they fit the available space.

3 Once all stitching is complete, finish your picture by mounting and framing (see page 101).

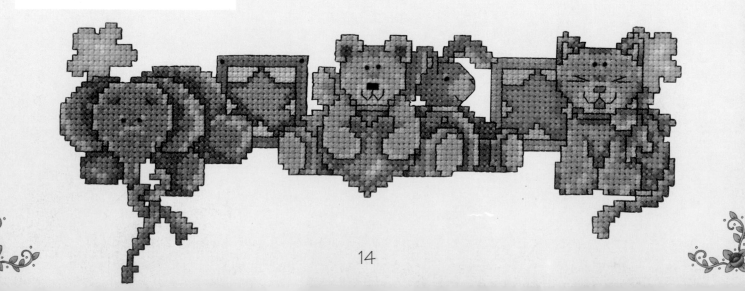

With
every little
baby's birth,
a
bit of heaven
drifts
to earth

Elizabeth
Anne
Newcombe
21 September
2004

Welcome Baby Cards

Stitch count (each card)
57h x 43w

❖

Design size (each card)
8 x 6cm (3¼ x 2⅜in)

Materials
(for each card)

21 x 19cm (8¼ x 7½in)
antique white 18-count Aida

❖

DMC stranded cotton (floss)
as listed in chart key

❖

Tapestry needle size 24

❖

Suitable card mount

1 Prepare for work, referring to Techniques if necessary. Find and mark the centre of the Aida fabric and circle the centre of the chart with a pen.

2 Start stitching from the centre of the chart and fabric, using two strands of stranded cotton (floss) for cross stitches. Following the chart for colour changes, work all French knots using two strands wrapped once around the needle and work all backstitches using one strand.

3 Once all the stitching is complete, mount your embroidery in a suitable card (see page 101 and also suggestions for decorating card mounts).

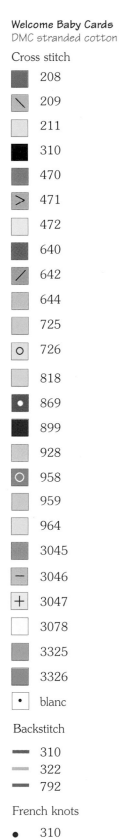

Welcome Baby Cards
DMC stranded cotton

Cross stitch

	208
\	209
	211
	310
	470
>	471
	472
	640
/	642
	644
	725
o	726
	818
⊙	869
	899
	928
⊙	958
	959
	964
	3045
−	3046
+	3047
	3078
	3325
	3326
•	blanc

Backstitch

—	310
—	322
—	792

French knots

●	310
○	725
●	958

Welcome Baby Sampler
DMC stranded cotton
Cross stitch

| 208 | 209 | 211 | 310 | 322 | 470 | 471 | 472 | 640 | 642 | 644 | 725 | 726 | 818 | 869 | 899 | 928 | 958 | 959 | 964 | 3045 |

Sound Advice

There are moments when we could all use some help getting through a busy day, when time is precious and household chores are last on our list of priorities. Place these four notices in the most important rooms in the house and deliver a smile to help cope with the demands of everyday life and make your tasks just a little lighter. The colourful designs are easy to stitch on 14-count Aida, using just cross stitch, backstitch and French knots.

Sound Advice

Stitch count (each notice)
98h x 70w

Design size (each notice)
18 x 13cm (7 x 5in)

Materials
(for each notice)

30.5 x 25.5cm (12 x 10in)
antique white 14-count Aida

DMC stranded cotton (floss)
as listed in chart key

Tapestry needle size 24

1 Prepare for work, referring to Techniques if necessary. Find and mark the centre of the fabric and circle the centre of the chart (pages 24–27) with a pen. Use an embroidery frame if you wish.

2 Start stitching from the centre of the chart and fabric. Work over one block of Aida, using two strands of stranded cotton (floss) for cross stitches and one strand for all the backstitches. Following the chart for colour changes, work all French knots using two strands wound once around the needle.

3 Once all stitching is complete, finish your picture by mounting and framing (see page 101).

Ward off the fussy eaters in the family with this no-nonsense cook's warning posted in the kitchen.

Drop a gentle hint to everyone that all can help when it comes to keeping the bathroom clean and tidy.

Declare the joys of organized chaos and celebrate your mess — perfect for a teen's bedroom or anyone's private space.

When dust bunnies are underfoot, this humorous advice for the living room will help you ignore them.

Sound Advice in the Kitchen
DMC stranded cotton

Cross stitch

◉	310
╱	312
	317
	318
	334
❙	350
	415
∧	725
	726
⌐	727
○	729
−	747
╱	762
	817
✕	818
	869
	899
	904
↓	906
	907
⊤	945
	951
▢	3326
	3755
✛	3829
→	3841
•	blanc

Backstitch

—	310
—	350
—	904

French knots

●	310

**Sound Advice
in the Bathroom**
DMC stranded cotton

Cross stitch

⊡	310
╱	312
	318
	334
I	350
	415
╲	676
∧	725
	726
⌐	727
○	729
−	747
╱	762
	817
✕	818
	869
	899
	904
↓	906
	907
T	945
	951
☐	3326
	3755
✛	3829
•	blanc

Backstitch
— 310
— 904

French knots
● 310
○ 726

**Sound Advice
in the Living Room**
DMC stranded cotton

Cross stitch

⊙	310
╱	312
	317
	318
	334
▮	350
	415
╲	676
∧	725
	726
˥	727
○	729
−	747
╱	762
	817
✕	818
	869
	899
	904
↓	906
	907
T	945
	951
▢	3326
✛	3829
•	blanc

Backstitch
— 310
— 334
— 904

French knots
● 310
● 899

Sound Advice in the Bedroom
DMC stranded cotton

Cross stitch

⊡	310
	318
	334
I	350
	415
\	676
∧	725
	726
⌐	727
O	729
−	747
/	762
	817
✕	818
	869
	899
	904
↓	906
	907
T	945
	951
▫	3326
	3755
+	3829
→	3841
•	blanc

Backstitch
—	310
—	334

French knots
●	310
●	3326

Celtic Spirit

Irish culture is rich with blessings that speak to the spirit with words of encouragement and hope. Each line of this benevolent proverb wishes an easy journey through life to those who read it. In keeping with the illuminated manuscripts of the Celts, an intricate knotwork border frames the words. In antique gold on a background of rich blues and greens, the intertwining cord takes a path with no beginning or end, the everlasting journey signifying the thread of a life connected to all living things. The hypnotic visual qualities of the intricate knotwork were said to lead the onlooker on a quest for spiritual growth.

The matching pincushion and sachet (overleaf) carry the same interlacing border design and make lovely tokens of affection for someone special. All three projects could also be stitched on a 14-count Aida fabric.

Celtic Spirit Sampler

Stitch count
224h x 168w

❈

Design size
40.5 x 30.5cm (16 x 12in)

Materials

53 x 43cm (21 x 17in) putty
28-count Cashel linen
(Zweigart #345)

❈

DMC stranded cotton (floss)
as listed in chart key

❈

Tapestry needle size 24

1 Prepare for work, referring to Techniques. Find and mark the centre of the fabric and centre of the chart (pages 32–35) with a pen. Use an embroidery frame if you wish.

2 Start stitching from the centre of the fabric and chart working over two fabric threads and using two strands of stranded cotton (floss) for cross stitches. Following the chart for colour changes, work French knots using two strands wound once around the needle. Use two strands of DMC 312 for backstitch lettering, one strand of DMC 833 for backstitch within the illuminated letters and one strand of black for all other outlines. If using Anchor colours, use 874 for DMC 833 and 907 for DMC 831.

3 Once the stitching is complete, finish your picture by mounting and framing (see page 101).

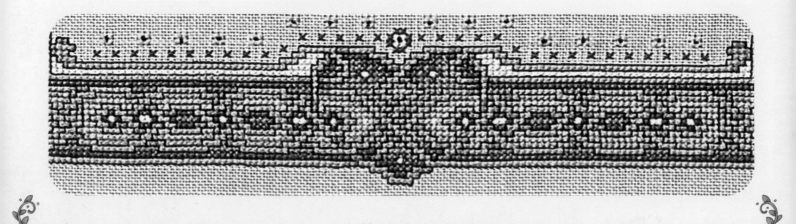

Celtic Spirit Pincushion

Stitch count
48h x 72w

Design size
8.7 x 13cm (3½ x 5in)

Materials

21 x 25cm (8½ x 10in) putty
28-count Cashel linen
(Zweigart #345)

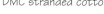

DMC stranded cotton (floss)
as listed in chart key

Tapestry needle size 24

21 x 25cm (8½ x 10in) lightweight
iron-on interfacing

21 x 25cm (8½ x 10in) backing
fabric to tone with embroidery

Polyester filling

61cm (24in) decorative braid
to tone with embroidery

Two small gold decorative
buttons or charms

1 Follow steps 1 and 2 of the sampler on page 28 but use one strand of black for all backstitches.

2 Once the embroidery is complete, place the iron-on interfacing over the wrong side of the embroidery and press to fuse, according to the manufacturer's instructions.

3 Pin the backing fabric and embroidery together, right sides facing. Mark a line along all sides, 2.5cm (1in) beyond the edge of the embroidery and then trim the layers along this line. Using matching thread, stitch a 1.25cm (½in) seam all around, leaving a gap for turning at the bottom. Turn through to the right side and stuff with polyester filling.

4 Attach the braid, starting at the gap and slipstitching it around all edges. Tuck the ends into the gap and slipstitch closed. Stitch on a decorative button or charm at the top and bottom centre.

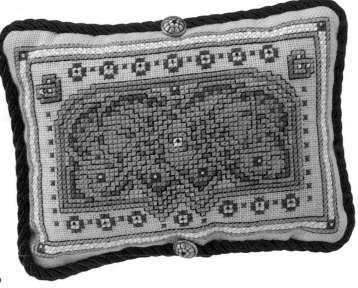

Pincushion and Sachet
DMC stranded cotton

Cross stitch

■	312	▨	833
╱	322	■	3802
□	334	•	blanc
■	502		
+	503	**Backstitch**	
■	504	—	310
∧	831		

French knots
● 310
○ blanc

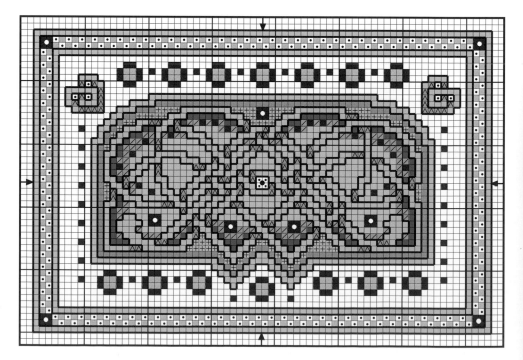

Celtic Spirit Sachet

Stitch count
74h x 66w

Design size
13.5 x 12cm (5¼ x 4¾in)

Materials

25 x 25cm (10 x 10in) putty
28-count Cashel linen
(Zweigart #345)

DMC stranded cotton (floss)
as listed in chart key

Tapestry needle size 24

25 x 25cm (10 x 10in)
lightweight iron-on interfacing

25 x 25cm (10 x 10in) backing
fabric to tone with embroidery

76cm (30in) decorative braid to
tone with embroidery

Polyester filling

51cm (20in) ribbon
9mm (⅜in) wide to tone
with decorative braid

Two small gold decorative
buttons or charms

Matching sewing thread

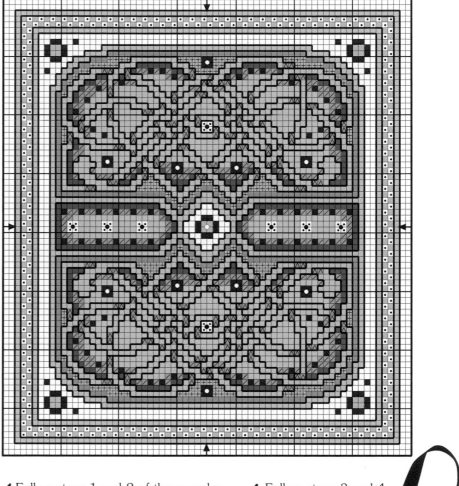

1 Follow steps 1 and 2 of the sampler on page 28 but use one strand of black for all backstitches. Use the chart above and key opposite.

2 Once the embroidery is complete, follow step 2 for the pincushion opposite.

3 Make a hanging loop by cutting the length of ribbon in half. Fold one piece in half lengthways and place it between the backing fabric and embroidery at the centre top, raw edges matching, with the loop towards the centre. Cut the other length of ribbon in half and place at the centre bottom in the same way.

4 Follow steps 3 and 4 of the pincushion to make up the sachet.

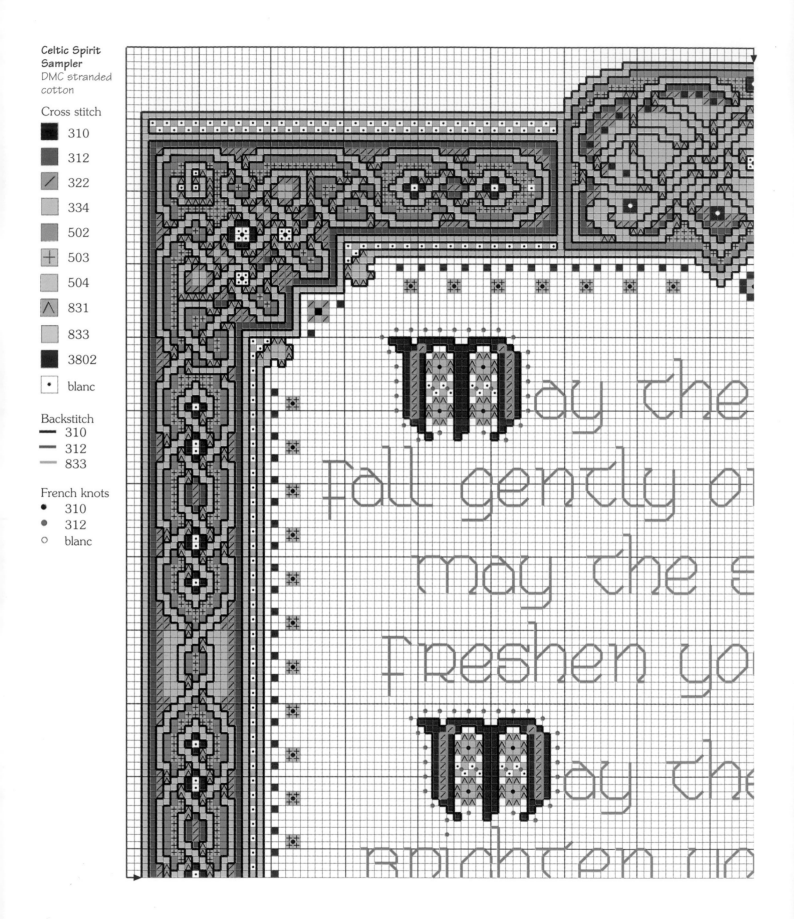

Cross stitch

■	310
■	312
/	322
▨	334
▨	502
+	503
▨	504
∧	831
▨	833
■	3802
⊡	blanc

Backstitch
— 310
— 312
— 833

French knots
● 310
● 312
○ blanc

raindrops
n your brow,
soft winds
ur Spirit.
e sunshine
rin heart

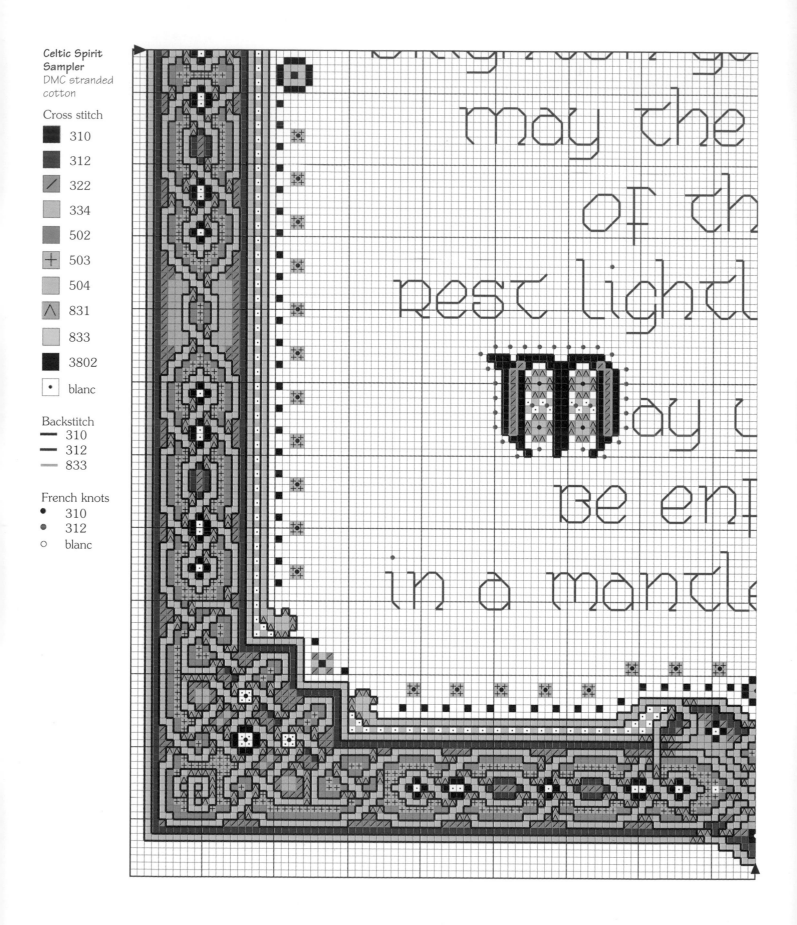

burdens
e day
y upon you.

your life
olded
e of **L**ove.

Home is Where Your Honey Is

Since the early 18th century, cross stitch samplers have been used to express the importance of home and family. Here is a lighthearted interpretation that draws on just those sentiments. Imagine the gentle hum of the bumblebee and a pot of honey to sweeten the day in a cosy setting for a teddy bear couple.

A palette of bright pastels adds to the romance these teddies share. Stitched on Fiddler's Light Aida fabric to add a homespun touch, the happy couple sit side by side with a sparkle in their eyes. They let us know that when a house is filled with love it can truly be called a home.

Stitch count
129h x 102w

Design size
23.5 x 18.5cm (9¼ x 7¼in)

Materials

36 x 31cm (14 x 12in)
Fiddler's Light 14-count Aida
(Charles Craft)

DMC stranded cotton (floss)
as listed in chart key

Tapestry needle size 24

1 Prepare for work, referring to Techniques if necessary. Find and mark the centre of the fabric and circle the centre of the chart with a pen. Mount your fabric in an embroidery frame if you wish.

2 Start stitching from the centre of the chart and fabric, using two strands of stranded cotton (floss) for cross stitches. Following the chart for colour changes, work all French knots using two strands wound once around the needle. Use two strands of DMC 3838 (or Anchor equivalent 177) for the backstitch lettering and one strand for all other backstitch outlines following the colour changes as indicated on the chart.

3 Once all stitching is complete, finish your picture by mounting and framing (see page 101).

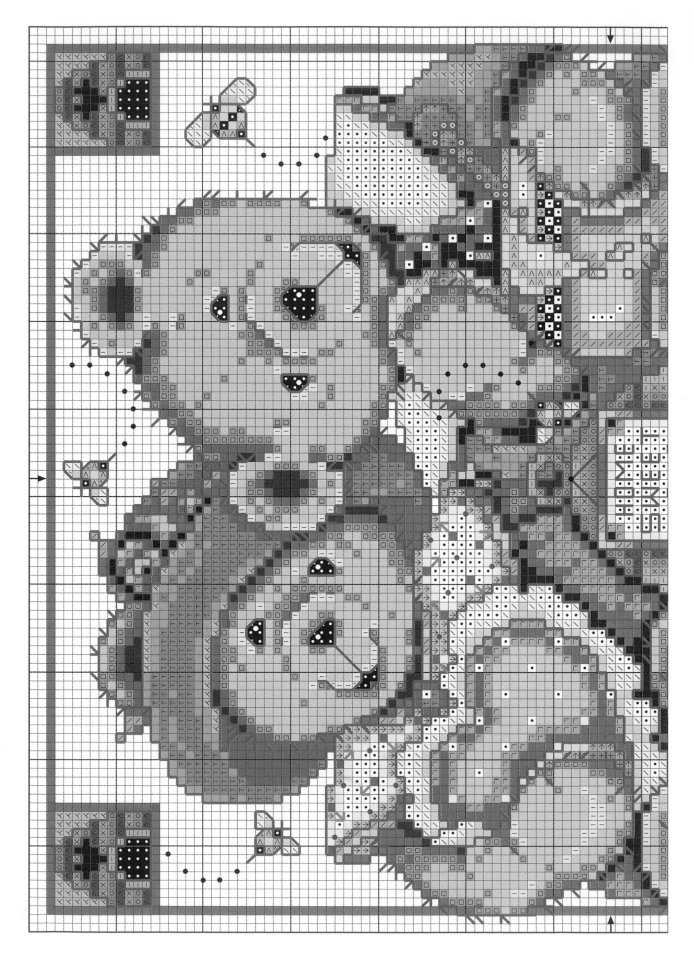

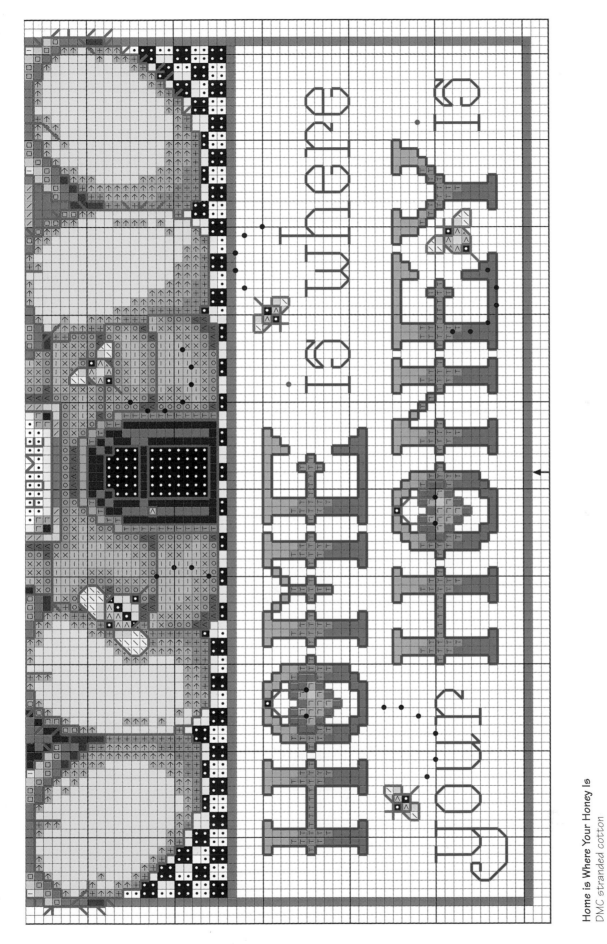

Home is Where Your Honey Is
DMC stranded cotton

Cross stitch

● 310	＋ 436	／ 472	／ 762
341	↑ 437	＞ 725	869
415	470	726	898
○ 434	／ 471	739	□ 3045

3046	— 3047	3687	ꀃ 3688
3689	＜ 3747	→ 3752	3753
3803	3820	✕ 3822	＜ 3829
3838	┬ 3839	○ 3852	● blanc

Backstitch
— 310
— 470
— 3838

French knots
● 310
● 3838
○ blanc

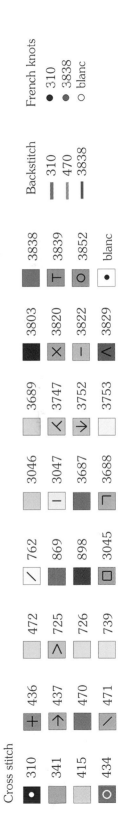

In the Garden

The cottage garden in this delightful sampler is filled with the sweet fragrance of flowers and the gentle melody of songbirds. The classic verse on the sampler celebrates that special place that all gardeners hold so dear. A place of glorious renewal, a sun-kissed garden is a haven to bunnies, butterflies and nests filled with eggs. In city or country, no matter how small, a garden always seems to bring the onlooker just a bit closer to heaven on Earth.

Pass on the pleasures of gardening to those you love with easy-to-stitch heart-shaped greeting cards. Using the same designs, you can quickly work up a set of plant pokes and add an affectionate note to your indoor garden.

Stitch count
130h x 102w

Design size
23.5 x 18.5cm (9¼ x 7¼in)

Materials

33.5 x 31cm (13¼ x 12¼in) Rustico 14-count Aida (Zweigart #54)

DMC stranded cotton (floss) as listed in chart key

Tapestry needle size 24

In the Garden Sampler

1 Prepare for work, referring to Techniques if necessary. Find and mark the centre of the fabric and circle the centre of the chart (pages 44–45) with a pen. Use an embroidery frame if you wish.

2 Start stitching from the centre of the chart and the centre of the fabric. Work over one block of Aida, using two strands of stranded cotton (floss) for the full cross stitches and three-quarter cross stitches. Following the chart for all the colour changes, work all French knots using two strands wrapped once around the needle and work all backstitches using one strand.

3 Once all stitching is complete, finish your picture by mounting and framing (see page 101).

The kiss of the sun
for pardon,
The song of the birds
for mirth.
One is closer to God
in a garden,
Than anywhere else
on Earth.

Plant Pokes

Stitch count (each poke)
38h x 58w

Design size (each poke)
6.9 x 10.5cm (2¾ x 4⅛in)

Materials
(for each poke)

20 x 28cm (8 x 11in) sheet of white 14-count plastic canvas

DMC stranded cotton (floss) as listed in chart key

Tapestry needle size 24

20 x 28cm (8 x 11in) white felt for backing

Permanent fabric glue

Two 30.5cm (12in) lengths of 1cm (3/16in) dowel, painted white

Assorted 20cm (8in) lengths of ribbon to tone with embroidery

1 Prepare the canvas by trimming rough edges. You can stitch both pokes on one sheet of canvas leaving at least two bars between designs.

2 Start stitching from the centre of each charted design, using three strands of stranded cotton (floss) for cross stitches. Work all French knots using two strands wrapped once around the needle and work all backstitches using one strand.

3 Once all the stitching is complete, back the plant pokes by gluing on white felt, keeping the glue within the edges of the embroidery. Cut out each poke leaving one row of plastic canvas around the design. Glue a length of white dowel to the centre back of the poke making sure it does not show above the top of the embroidery. Using assorted coloured ribbons, cut four pieces in various lengths and tie one in a bow.
Glue the ribbons to the dowel below the embroidery, as shown below.

Plant Pokes and Cards
DMC stranded cotton

Cross stitch		Backstitch	
■	309	▬	309 pink heart outline
-	312	▬	310
╱	335	▬	312 blue heart letters
	340	▬	469
	470	▬	792 pink heart letters
	792	▬	931 blue heart outline
I	818		
	819	**French knots**	
	3326	●	310
I	3746	●	312 blue heart i dot
-	3752	●	340
	3753	●	792 pink heart i dot

Cards

To stitch the designs as cards, work them on 18 x 21cm (7 x 8¼in) pieces of white 18-count Aida following the stitching instructions in step 2 of the sampler on page 40. Mount the embroidery into a card. Stitch counts 38h x 58w and design sizes 5.4 x 8.2cm (2⅛ x 3¼in).

In the Garden
DMC stranded cotton

Cross stitch

Colour	Symbol
304	◣
309	◼
310	◼•
312	◼
320	✕
341	⌄
368	⌐
415	◼
420	◼
743	◼
745	◼
762	I
776	–
792	∕
793	+
801	❙
818	◼
899	◼
986	O
3045	◼
3046	＜
3047	◼
3346	◼
3347	＼
3348	◼
3766	◼
3811	◼
3823	O
3841	◼
blanc	•

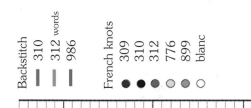

Backstitch
- 310
- 312 words
- 986

French knots
- 309
- 310
- 312
- 776
- 899
- blanc

Help Wanted

If it seems that there is a shortage of help around the house lately, this Help Wanted poster may be just what you have been looking for. Bright colours and smiling teddy bears lend a cheerfully gentle note to your requests for everyone to pitch in and keep the household running smoothly. Whether it's tidying up their room, answering the telephone, or making sure they don't bring the rainy day into the house, the entire family will be 'on notice'. Once the day is through it is time to remember the most important rule of all, to love one another – for it's love that makes a house a home. The individual motifs in this design could also be stitched separately to create a wealth of quick projects, such as small pictures or cards.

Stitch count
323h x 113w

Design size
58.5cm x 20.5cm (23 x 8in)

Materials

71 x 33cm (28 x 13in) Fiddler's Light 14-count Aida (Charles Craft)

DMC stranded cotton (floss) as listed in chart key

Tapestry needle size 24

1 Prepare your fabric for work, referring to Techniques if necessary. Find and mark the centre of the fabric and circle the centre of the chart with a pen. Use an embroidery frame if you wish.

2 Start stitching from the centre of the chart and fabric, using two strands of stranded cotton (floss) for full cross stitches and three-quarter cross stitches. Following the chart for colour changes, work all French knots using two strands wrapped once around the needle and work all backstitches using one strand. Use the alphabet charted on page 98 to stitch

the name of your choice. Plan the letters carefully on graph paper first to ensure they fit the space, remembering the spaces between the letters. If the name is a long one you can omit the four rosebud motifs.

3 Once all stitching is complete, finish your picture by mounting and framing (see page 101).

Help Wanted
DMC stranded cotton

Cross stitch

208	209	211	221	310	311	312	318	334	349	350	414	415	434	436	469	470	471	676	677	725	726	729	741
	X		O	•	I		>	/	<				<				+		I	△	O		

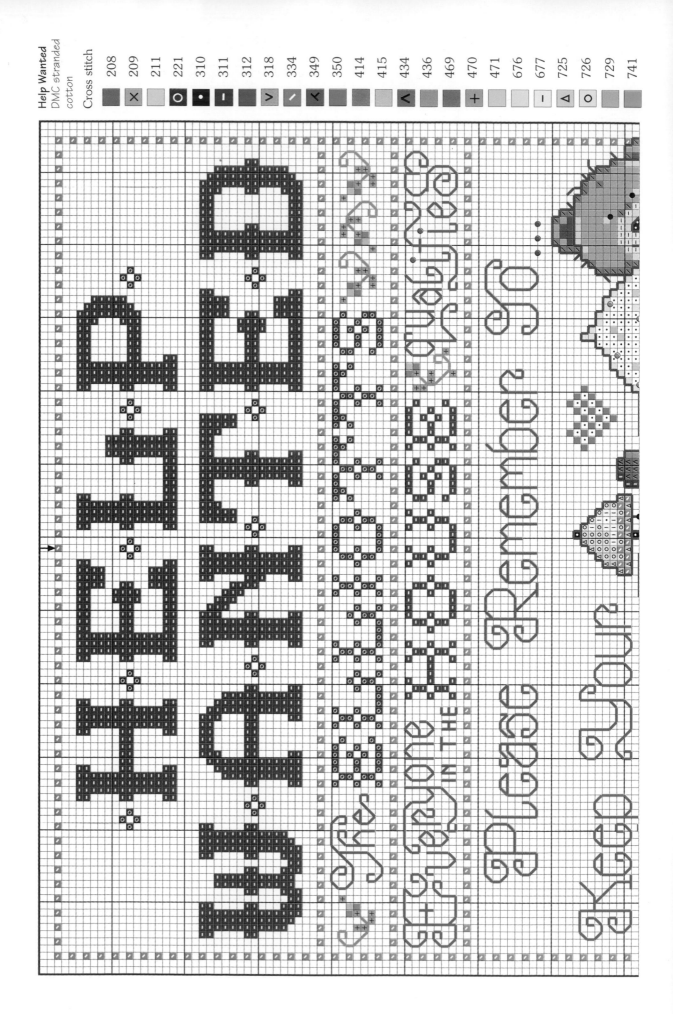

Help Wanted
DMC stranded cotton

Cross stitch

| 208 | 209 | 211 | 221 | 310 | 311 | 312 | 318 | 334 | 349 | 350 | 414 | 415 | 434 | 436 | 469 | 470 | 471 | 676 | 677 | 725 | 726 | 729 | 741 |

50

| 742 | 747 | 762 | 801 | 816 | 818 | 869 | 899 | 3078 | 3326 | 3755 | 3829 | 3841 | blanc | Backstitch | 221 | 310 | 311 | 469 | French knots | 208 | 221 | 310 | 311 | 899 | blanc |

Be as the dragonfly,
soar on your Dreams;
Be as the water,
reflect Beauty;
Be as the seasons,
open to Change;
Be as the wind,
refresh your Spirit;
Be as the blossom,
open to Joy.

Wisdom of the East

The aesthetic beauty of Asian culture is brought to life in this lovely sampler. The words express our close connection to nature, encouraging us to embrace the life force in all living things.

The peonies, irises and orchids represent the beauty, love and joy we see around us every day while dragonflies drift by and koi shimmer like precious gems in the water.

Using the gold borders as a guide, the individual vignettes can be stitched separately to create projects such as bookmarks, sachets and cards.

Card

Stitch this pretty peony card using the chart on page 59, centring the motif on a 19 x 21cm (7½ x 8¼in) piece of Fiddler's Light 18-count Aida and following the stitching instructions in step 2 of the sampler overleaf. Mount the embroidery in a suitable card (see page 101). Stitch count 43h x 57w and design size 6 x 8cm (2⅜ x 3⅛in).

Wisdom of the East Sampler

Stitch count
225h x 169w

Design size
41 x 31cm (16 x 12in)

Materials

53 x 43cm (21 x 17in) platinum 28-count Cashel linen (Zweigart #770)

DMC stranded cotton (floss) as listed in chart key

Kreinik #4 braid 028 citron

Mill Hill petite glass beads 42014 black

Tapestry needle size 24 and a beading needle

1 Prepare for work, referring to Techniques if necessary. Find and mark the centre of the fabric and chart. Use a frame if you wish.

2 Start stitching from the centre of the chart and fabric, working over two fabric threads and using two strands of stranded cotton (floss) for full cross stitches and three-quarter cross stitches and one strand of Kreinik #4 braid 028 for gold metallic cross stitches. Work French knots using two strands wrapped once around the needle and backstitches using one strand. Attach black petite glass beads where indicated on the chart, using a beading needle and matching thread (see page 101).

3 Once all stitching is complete, finish your picture by mounting and framing (see page 101).

Bookmark

Make a pretty bookmark, using the main chart, stitching the motifs on a 28 x 20.5cm (11 x 8in) piece of Fiddler's Light 18-count Aida and following step 2 of the sampler above. Trim the finished embroidery eight rows beyond the design and create a fringe with a machine stitch in toning thread, three rows beyond the embroidery all round. Pull out the threads up to the stitching line. Cut a piece of fusible web and white felt the same size as the finished design. Place the web on the back of the design, then the felt and iron to fuse. Stitch count 122h x 32w and design size 17 x 4.5cm (7 x 2in).

Bowl

Stitch this fan motif from the main chart to decorate a bowl lid (Framecraft code W4E). Work on a 20 x 20cm (8 x 8in) piece of platinum 28-count Cashel linen and follow the stitching instructions in step 2 of the sampler opposite. Mount the finished embroidery into the bowl lid according to the manufacturer's instructions. Glue decorative black braid around the outer rim and tie in a knot, then attach a bead and tassel to each end. Stitch count 42h x 40w and design size 7.5 x 7.5cm (3 x 3in).

Sachet

Stitch count
43h x 87w

Design size
7.8 x 15.8cm (3 x 6¼in)

Materials

20 x 28cm (8 x 11in) platinum 28-count Cashel linen (Zweigart #770)

DMC stranded cotton (floss) as listed in chart key

Kreinik #4 braid 028 citron

Tapestry needle size 24

Lightweight iron-on interfacing

23cm (¼yd) fabric for backing

Polyester filling

30cm (12in) of 5mm (¼in) wide black satin ribbon

91cm (1yd) decorative black braid, two decorative buttons and one small black tassel

1 Use the main chart to stitch the motif, following the instructions in step 2 of the sampler opposite.

2 Make up into a sachet. Trim the linen ten rows beyond the design and press iron-on interfacing the same size on to the wrong side.

3 Make a hanging loop by folding the ribbon in half lengthways and pinning it centrally on the right side, loop down, raw edges matching. Cut backing fabric to match the embroidery and pin in place, right sides facing. Using matching sewing thread, stitch a 1.25cm (½in) seam all around, securing the loop and leaving an opening at the bottom. Turn through and stuff with filling.

4 Slipstitch the braid around all edges, beginning at centre bottom. Tuck it into the gap, attach the tassel and slipstitch closed. Sew on decorative buttons at centre top and bottom.

55

Wisdom of the East
DMC stranded cotton

Cross stitch

☒ 309	340	470	⟍ 504	△ 729	818	3811	3853
⊡ 310	⌐ 341	⊙ 471	− 597	− 746	⟍ 869	∧ 3820	3854
⁄ 312	415	472	598	⏐ 762	899	3822	• blanc
318	433	502	676	775	⊙ 3325	✚ 3829	☒ Kreinik No.4
334	⁄ 469	503	677	776	⏐ 3746	3852	Braid 028

Backstitch

— 310
— 312
— 472
— Kreinik No.4
Braid 028

French knots

● 310
● 312
● 341
● 469

Mill Hill beads

◎ 42014 black

Wisdom of the East
DMC stranded cotton

Cross stitch

☒ 309	▨ 340	▨ 470	◣ 504	△ 729	▨ 818	▨ 3811	▨ 3853
⊡ 310	⌐ 341	○ 471	− 597	− 746	◣ 869	▨ 3820	▨ 3854
◢ 312	▨ 415	472	598	Ⅰ 762	▨ 899	3822	• blanc
▨ 318	▨ 433	▨ 502	676	775	○ 3325	▨ 3829	☒ Kreinik No.4
▨ 334	◢ 469	▨ 503	677	776	Ⅰ 3746	▨ 3852	Braid 028

Backstitch

— 310
— 312
— 472
— Kreinik No.4
Braid 028

French knots

● 310
● 312
○ 341
● 469

Mill Hill beads

◉ 42014 black

Sweet Sentiments

Greetings cards are a wonderful way to send heart-felt sentiments to those we care about. Whether in traditional sampler form or with a whimsical illustration, this collection of cards is sure to provide just the right words for special occasions. Send a birthday wish with words for a happy heart. Two charming teddy bears will help express your thanks for someone's good deed. Encourage a worthy effort or special achievement with the old adage 'practice makes perfect'. Let both your parents know just how wonderful you think they are and say hello to a friend far away by letting them know they are in your heart.

Sweet Sentiments Cards

Stitch count (each card)
57h x 43w

Design size (each card)
8 x 6cm (3⅛ x 2⅜in)

Materials

(for each card)

21.5 x 19cm (8½ x 7½in)
Fiddler's Light 18-count Aida
(Charles Craft)

DMC stranded cotton (floss)
as listed in chart key

Tapestry needle size 24

Suitable card mount

1 Prepare for work, referring to Techniques if necessary. Find and mark the centre of the fabric and circle the centre of the chart (pages 62–65) with a pen.

2 Start stitching from the centre of the chart and fabric, using two strands of stranded cotton (floss) for full and three-quarter cross stitches. Work French knots using two strands wrapped once around the needle and backstitches using one strand.

3 Once all the stitching is complete, mount your embroidery in a suitable card (see page 101 and also suggestions for decorating card mounts).

Happy Birthday (below)
DMC stranded cotton

Cross stitch

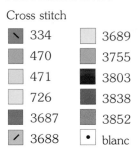

◣	334			3689
	470			3755
	471			3803
	726			3838
	3687			3852
◿	3688	•		blanc

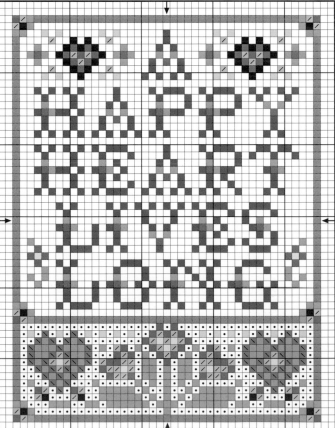

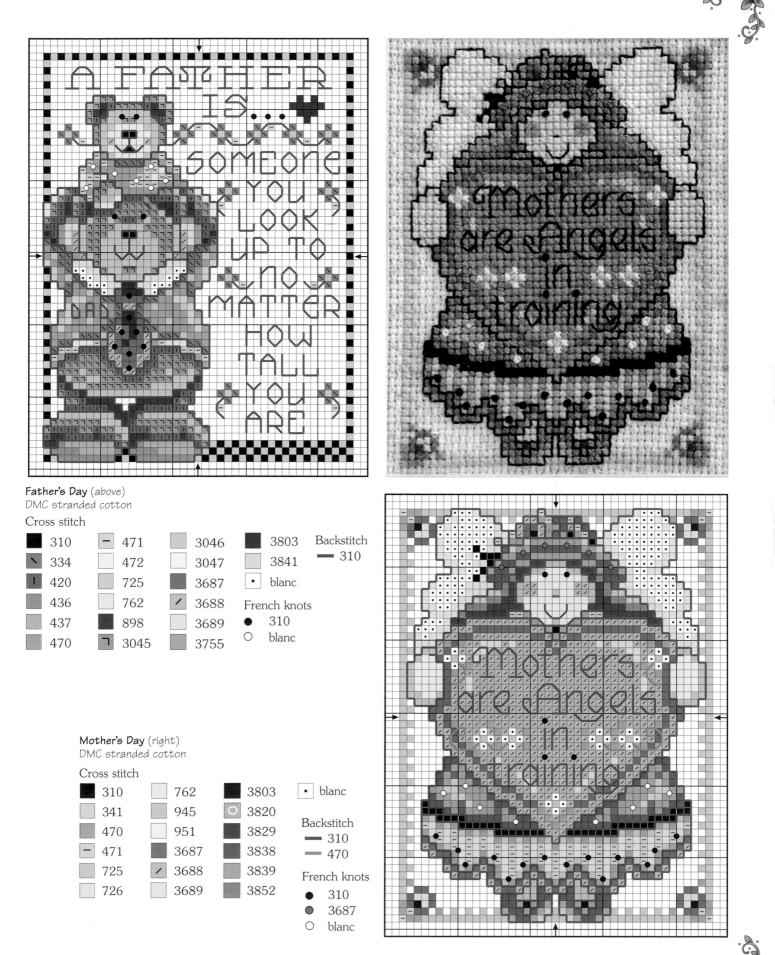

Father's Day (above)
DMC stranded cotton

Cross stitch

■ 310	− 471	3046	■ 3803	**Backstitch**		
◤ 334	472	3047	3841	— 310		
▮ 420	725	3687	• blanc			
436	762	╱ 3688		**French knots**		
437	■ 898	3689	● 310			
470	⌐ 3045	3755	○ blanc			

Mother's Day (right)
DMC stranded cotton

Cross stitch

■ 310	762	■ 3803	• blanc	
341	945	◉ 3820		
470	951	3829	**Backstitch**	
− 471	3687	3838	— 310	
725	╱ 3688	3839	— 470	
726	3689	3852		

French knots
● 310
● 3687
○ blanc

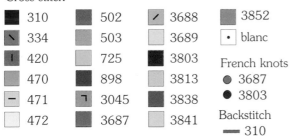

Missing You (*above*)
DMC stranded cotton

Cross stitch

■ 310	■ 502	✔ 3688	■ 3852	
✖ 334	■ 503	3689	· blanc	
▮ 420	725	■ 3803		
■ 470	■ 898	3813	**French knots**	
— 471	⌐ 3045	3838	● 3687	
472	■ 3687	■ 3841	● 3803	

Backstitch
—— 310

Thank You (*above*)
DMC stranded cotton

Cross stitch

◼ 310	725	3687	3838	**Backstitch**	
341	726	╱ 3688	3839	— 310	
▮ 420	762	3689	3852	— 3838	
470	◼ 898	◼ 3803	• blanc	**French knots**	
— 471	⌐ 3045	⊙ 3820		● 310	
472	3046	3821		● 3838	

Practice Makes Perfect (*left*)
DMC stranded cotton

Cross stitch

470	3689	**Backstitch**	
— 471	3838	— 310	
502	3839	— 470	
503	3852		
3687	• blanc		
╱ 3688			

All in a Day's Work

These days the daily routines at work can often seem overwhelming and a sense of humour can help us through the more trying moments. Posted close by your desk, these three notices can help everyday frustrations melt away in a smile. When the clock is ticking, deadlines looming and everyone is in a rush, let them know you are working as fast as you can. If papers are piled high and quitting time draws near, thank goodness you somehow always manage to squeeze hours of work into those last precious minutes. Most importantly, don't forget to take a break and spare a few moments for a well-deserved daydream. After all, the work will be waiting when you return.

All in a Day's Work

1 Prepare for work, referring to Techniques if necessary. Find and mark the centre of the fabric and circle the centre of the chart with a pen. Mount the fabric in an embroidery frame if you wish.

2 Start stitching from the centre of the chart and fabric, using two strands of stranded cotton (floss) for full cross stitches and three-quarter cross stitches. Following the chart for colour changes, work all French knots using two strands wrapped once around the needle and work all backstitches using one strand.

3 Once all stitching is complete, finish your picture by mounting and framing (see page 101).

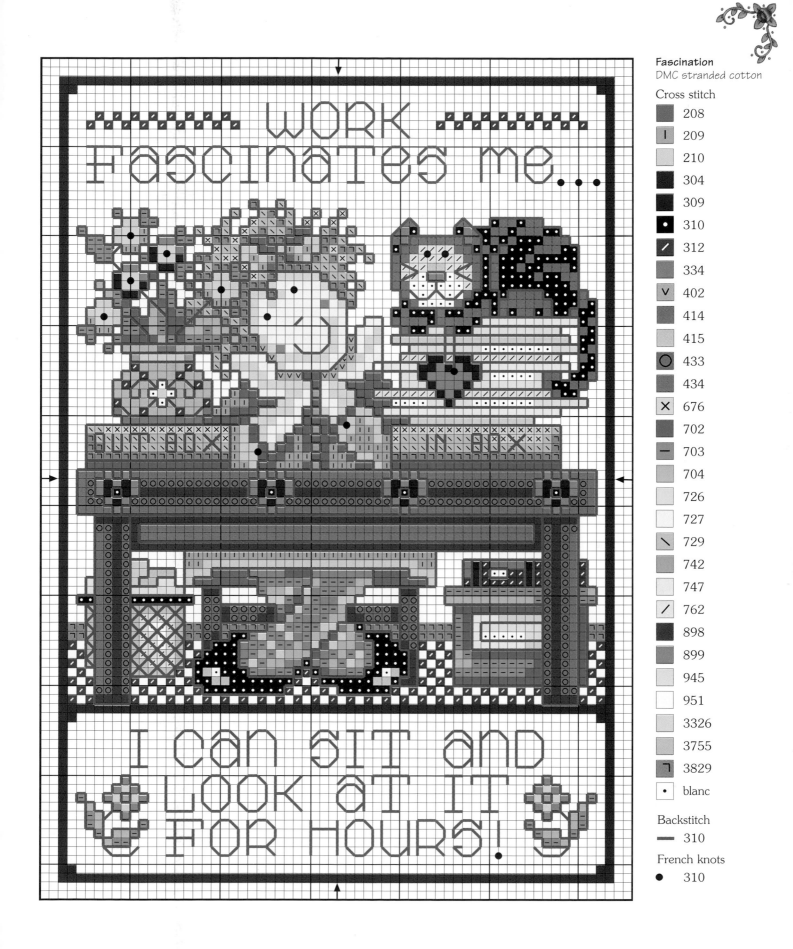

Fascination
DMC stranded cotton

Cross stitch

▨	208
I	209
	210
■	304
■	309
●	310
╱	312
	334
V	402
▨	414
	415
○	433
▨	434
✕	676
▨	702
—	703
	704
	726
	727
╲	729
▨	742
	747
╱	762
■	898
▨	899
	945
	951
	3326
	3755
ꓕ	3829
•	blanc

Backstitch
— 310

French knots
● 310

69

Mistakes
DMC stranded cotton

Cross stitch

◼	304
◼	309
◼•	310
╱	312
◼	334
◼	415
◯	433
◼	434
✕	676
◼	702
−	703
◼	704
◼	726
◼	727
◼	729
╲	742
◼	747
╱	762
✚	869
◼	898
◼	899
◼	945
◻	951
◼	3326
◼	3755
◤	3829
•	blanc

Backstitch
— 309
— 310

French knots
● 310

Wedding Wishes

Fairy roses and tender hearts in the softest
pink combine with the palest lavender lace to
frame a loving keepsake for a newly wed couple.
Worked on 28-count evenweave and embellished
with pink and white pearl seed beads,
the simple yet poignant verse echoes the
lasting vow of commitment the two have made
to each other. Presented on their wedding day,
this personalized sampler will be a lasting
treasure for the years to come. The design
could also be stitched on a 14-count Aida.
Carrying two bands of gold, the matching
ring pillow bestows a blessing of love on the
bride and groom. This pillow, edged in seed
pearls and lace, makes a beautiful
remembrance. The rings are held securely
in place with a small satin bow.

Wedding Ring Pillow

Stitch count
105h x 105w

Design size
15 x 15cm (5¾ x 5¾in)

Materials

27.5 x 27.5cm (10¼ x 10¾in)
antique white 18-count Aida

DMC stranded cotton (floss)
as listed in chart key

Mill Hill antique glass beads,
coral reef 03018 and
petite glass beads, white 40479

Tapestry needle size 24 and a
beading needle

23cm (¼yd) lightweight iron-on
interfacing

23cm (¼yd) white silk backing fabric

Polyester filling

91cm (1yd) decorative lace and
137cm (1½yd) pearl beading

25.5cm (10in) white satin ribbon
and four satin roses

Permanent fabric glue

1 Prepare for work, marking the centre of the fabric and chart. Use an embroidery frame if you wish. The chart could be enlarged on a colour photocopier if desired.

2 Start stitching from the centre of the chart and fabric, using two strands of stranded cotton (floss) for cross stitches. Work French knots with one strand wrapped twice around the needle and backstitches with one strand. Attach the beads (see page 101) where indicated on the chart, using a beading needle and matching thread.

3 Once all stitching is complete, make up into a pillow. Trim the embroidery leaving twelve rows beyond the edge all around. Cut iron-on interfacing to the same size and press on to the wrong side of the embroidery. Cut the backing fabric to the same size as the trimmed embroidery and pin in place, right

sides facing. Using matching sewing thread, stitch a 1.25cm (½in) seam all around, leaving an opening at the bottom for turning through. Turn through to the right side and stuff with polyester filling. Slipstitch the bottom opening closed.

4 Starting at one corner, slipstitch the lace close to the edge of the Aida, gathering it slightly as you turn the corners and overlapping where the ends meet. Using a very thin line of fabric glue, attach the pearl beading to the inner edge of the lace. Cut the remaining beading into eight equal pieces. Glue two lengths together at the centre, creating four decorations and attach at each corner of the pillow. Glue a rose to each corner.

5 Fold the satin ribbon in half and tack (baste) to the pillow, just above the centre heart on the inner border of the embroidery. Add the wedding rings and tie in a bow.

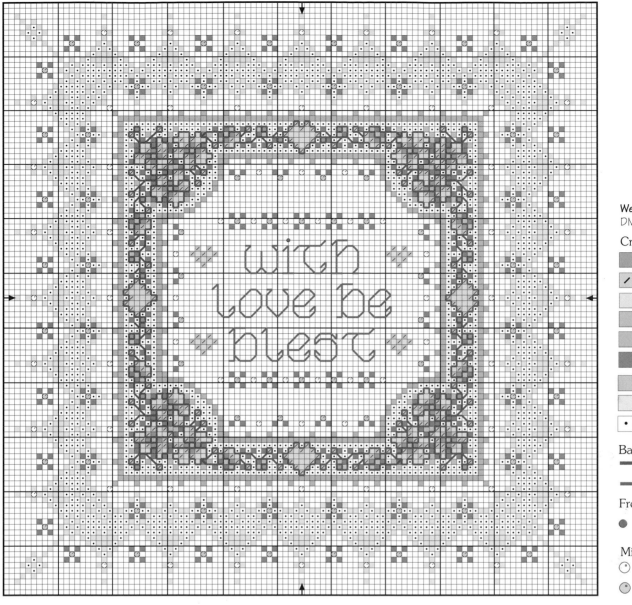

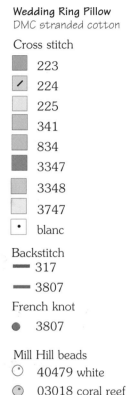

Wedding Ring Pillow
DMC stranded cotton

Cross stitch

▨	223
◪	224
☐	225
▨	341
▨	834
▨	3347
▨	3348
☐	3747
·	blanc

Backstitch

— 317
— 3807

French knot

● 3807

Mill Hill beads

⊙ 40479 white
◉ 03018 coral reef

Stitch count
129h x 129w

✿

Design size
23.5 x 23.5cm (9¼ x 9¼in)

Materials

33.5cm (13¼ x 13¼in) antique
white 28-count evenweave

✿

DMC stranded cotton (floss)
as listed in chart key

✿

Mill Hill antique glass beads, coral
reef 03018 and glass seed beads,
white 00479

✿

Tapestry needle size 24 and a
beading needle

Wedding Sampler

1 Prepare for work, referring to Techniques if necessary. Find and mark the centre of the fabric and chart (pages 76–77) with a pen. Use an embroidery frame if you wish.

2 Start stitching from the centre of the fabric and chart (overleaf), working over two threads and using two strands of stranded cotton (floss) for all cross stitches. Work all French knots using one strand wrapped twice around the needle and work all backstitches using one strand.

Use the alphabet on page 98 to stitch your names and dates. Plan the letters on graph paper first to ensure they fit the space. Finally, attach the beads (see page 101), using a beading needle and matching thread.

3 Once all stitching is complete, finish your picture by mounting and framing (see page 101).

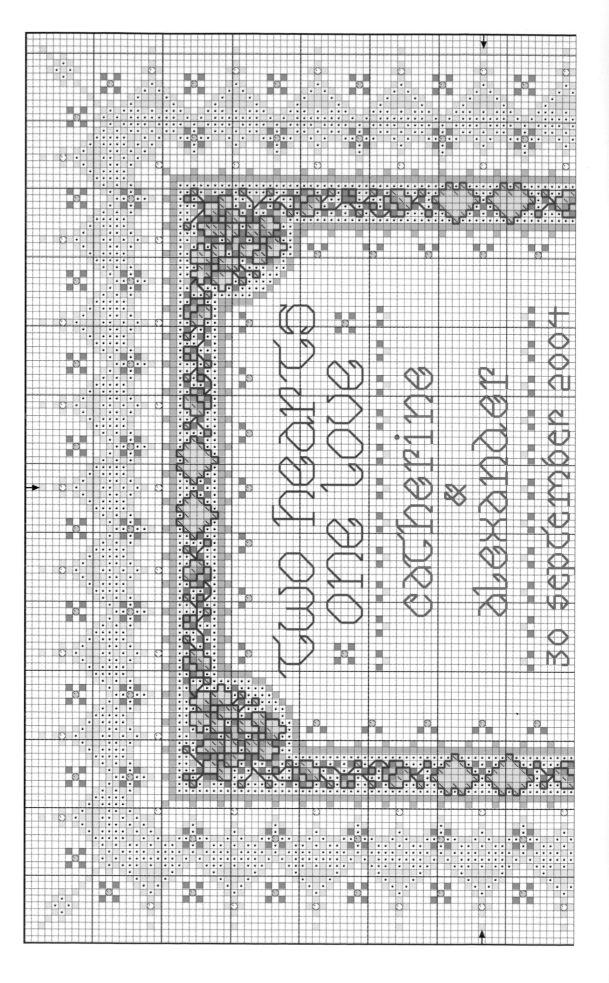

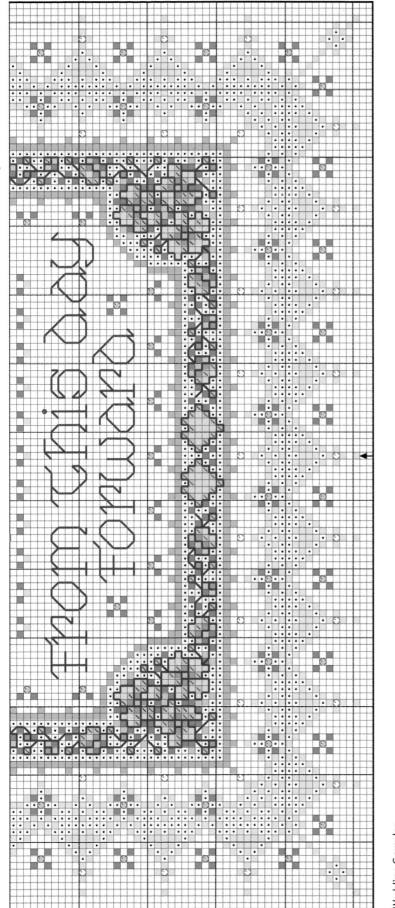

Wedding Sampler
DMC stranded cotton

Cross stitch

223	341	3348
224	834	3747
225	3347	• blanc

Backstitch
— 317
— 3807

French knots
● 317
● 3807

Mill Hill beads
⊙ 00479 white
◉ 03018 coral reef

Pure Indulgence

Rollick in the realm of life's sweetest pleasures with this carefree look at those little temptations we all try so hard to resist. With a palette of sweet-shop colours and a wink of good humour, these notices acknowledge those moments when we can no longer avoid the irresistible. If you have ever strayed from a diet or joyfully indulged in the scrumptious pleasure of a huge ice-cream soda or a delicious sundae, remember that sometimes too much of a good thing can be wonderful!

If you are counting calories and could use some help staying on task, try the three fridge magnets to provide words of encouragement. These three little helpers can also be stitched up as greetings cards to support a friend in resisting temptation.

Too much of
a good thing
can be...
wonderful

A balanced
diet is
a cookie in
each hand

Lead me
not into
temptation...
I already
know the way!

Fridge pickers
wear
big knickers

Pure Indulgence Notices

Stitch count (each notice)
88h x 60w

Design size (each notice)
11cm x 16cm (4¼ x 6¼in)

Materials
(for each notice)

23.5 x 28.5cm (9¼ x 11¼in)
Fiddler's Light 14-count Aida
(Charles Craft)

DMC stranded cotton (floss)
as listed in chart key

Tapestry needle size 24

1 Prepare for work, referring to Techniques if necessary. Find and mark the centre of the fabric and circle the centre of the chart (pages 82–84) with a pen. Use an embroidery frame if you wish.

2 Start stitching from the centre of the chart and fabric, using two strands of stranded cotton (floss) for full cross stitches and three-quarter cross stitches. Following the chart for colour changes, work all French knots using two strands wrapped once around the needle and work all backstitches using one strand.

3 Once all stitching is complete, finish your picture by mounting and framing (see page 101).

Fridge Magnets

Stitch count (each magnet)
41h x 41w

Design size (each magnet)
7.5 x 7.5cm (3 x 3in)

Materials
(for each magnet)

20 x 28cm (8 x 11in) sheet of
white 14-count plastic canvas

DMC stranded cotton (floss)
as listed in chart key

Tapestry needle size 24

25.5 x 30.5cm (10 x 12in)
self-adhesive photo magnet sheet
(from craft and stationery shops)

1 Prepare the canvas by trimming any rough edges. You can stitch all three magnets on one sheet of canvas leaving at least two bars between designs.

2 Start stitching from the centre of the chart on page 85, using three strands of stranded cotton (floss) for cross stitches. Work French knots using two strands wrapped once around the needle and backstitches using one strand of black.

3 Once all stitching is complete, cut out the design leaving one row of plastic canvas all round. Cut a 7.5cm (3in) diameter circle of self-adhesive photo magnet sheet for each magnet, and press on to the back of the embroidery.

Cards

Stitch count (each card)
41h x 41w

❊

Design size (each card)
6 x 6cm (2¼ x 2¼in)

Materials
(for each card)

18.5 x 18.5cm (7¼ x 7¼in) white
18-count Aida

❊

DMC stranded cotton (floss)
as listed in chart key

❊

Tapestry needle size 24

❊

Suitable card mount

1 Prepare for work. Start stitching from the centre of the design (charts on page 85), centring it on the fabric. Use two strands of stranded cotton (floss) for cross stitches. Work French knots with two strands wrapped once around the needle and backstitches with one strand of black.

2 Once all stitching is complete, mount your embroidery in a suitable card (see page 101, with suggestions for decorating cards).

A Good Thing
DMC stranded cotton

Cross stitch

208	I 318	I 434	\ 729	907	**Backstitch**
- 209	326	+ 436	742	v 3326	— 310
210	334	T 437	O 816	3829	**French knots**
309	335	676	818	• blanc	● 309
310	- 349	677	869		● 310
312	/ 350	× 725	905		○ 725
317	415	726	⨯ 906		

Temptation

DMC stranded cotton

Cross stitch

■	208	I 434	\ 729	V 3326			
−	209	+ 436	◉ 816		3755		
	210	T 437		818		3829	
■	312		676	■ 869		3841	
	335		677		905	• blanc	
−	349	× 725	∠ 906				
/	350		726		907		

Backstitch
— 310

French knots
● 310
◐ 726
○ blanc

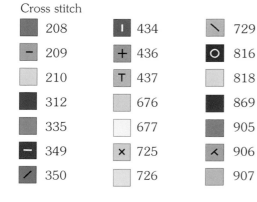

One Scoop
DMC stranded cotton

Cross stitch

■	309	▨	415	◪	839	▨	3829
■	312	▨	676	■	840	•	blanc
■	317	▨	677	▨	905		
▨	318	▨	729	◪	906		
■	326	▨	762	▨	907		
▨	335	▨	818	▨	3326		

Backstitch
— 310
— 312

French knots
● 312
○ blanc

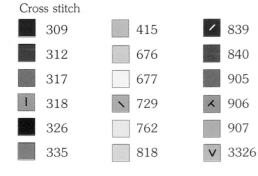

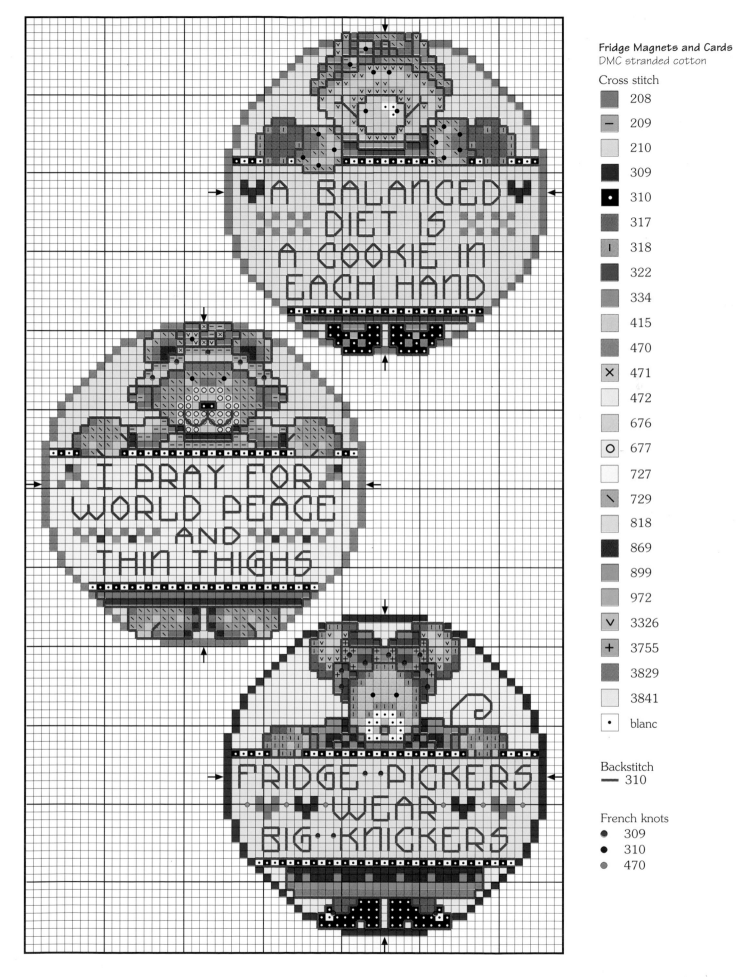

Fridge Magnets and Cards
DMC stranded cotton

Cross stitch

208
— 209
210
309
• 310
317
I 318
322
334
415
470
× 471
472
676
O 677
727
\ 729
818
869
899
972
∨ 3326
+ 3755
3829
3841
• blanc

Backstitch
— 310

French knots
● 309
● 310
● 470

Heart Strings

Fanciful angels surrounded by borders of hearts and flowers convey messages of love and kind deeds on these three charming hangings.

With a teddy in her arms, one angel reminds us that a hug is just the right size for everyone to receive while another angel encourages us to take heed of the little loving things we can do to help others. Hearts and flowers help two tiny angels herald the oft-quoted scripture, 'Love is patient, love is kind'.

You can make up these designs either on felt or as small stuffed pillows, all with ribbons for hanging, ready to place anywhere you wish to deliver an extra sprinkling of love.

Heart Strings Felt Hangings

Stitch count
62h x 62w

Design size
11.2 x 11.2cm (4½ x 4½in)

Materials
(for each hanging)

24 x 24cm (9½ x 9½in) white
14-count Aida

DMC stranded cotton (floss)
as listed in chart key

Tapestry needle size 24

13 x 13cm (5 x 5in) heavy
white card

Two 18 x 18cm (7 x 7in) pieces
of medium-weight, iron-on
interfacing

Two 18 x 18cm (7 x 7in) pieces of
felt to tone with embroidery

Fusible web (Steam-A-Seam 2 –
see Suppliers)

46cm (18in) ribbon 1cm (¼in) wide
to tone with embroidery

Four decorative satin roses

Permanent fabric glue

1 Prepare for work, referring to Techniques if necessary. Find and mark the centre of the fabric and chart. Use an embroidery frame if you wish. Please note: a single key has been used for all three designs but you may not need all of the colours for each design.

2 Start stitching from the centre of the fabric and chart (overleaf), using two strands of stranded cotton (floss) for full cross stitches and three-quarter cross stitches. Work French knots using two strands wrapped once around the needle and backstitches using one strand.

3 Once the stitching is complete, make up into a felt hanging as follows. Trim the embroidery ten rows beyond the design. Fold the edges to the back leaving a four-row border all around and press the folds. Trim the heavy card to fit behind the embroidery under the folded edges. Glue the edges to the back of the card with permanent fabric glue.

4 Press a piece of iron-on interfacing to each piece of felt, interfacing side up, and cut a piece of fusible web to match the felt size. Place this on top and add the second piece of felt, interfacing side down. Using a press cloth, iron to fuse the layers, leaving the top edge open.

5 For a decorative effect, use pinking shears all around the felt close to the edge. Cut the length of ribbon in half and position the two lengths 4.5cm (1¾in) from either side of the felt, inserting it 2.5cm (1in) between the layers. Iron to fuse the top edge. Apply permanent fabric glue sparingly to the back of the embroidery close to the edge. Position the embroidery centrally on the felt, making sure that no glue oozes out. Glue a satin rose to each corner. Tie the ribbons in a bow to create a hanger.

Heart Strings Pillow Hangings

1 Prepare for work, referring to Techniques if necessary. Find and mark the centre of the fabric and chart. Use an embroidery frame if you wish. Please note: a single key has been used for all three designs but you may not need all of the colours for each design.

2 Start stitching from the centre of the fabric and chart (overleaf), using two strands of stranded cotton (floss) for full cross stitches and three-quarter cross stitches. Work French knots using two strands wrapped once around the needle and backstitches using one strand.

3 Once the stitching is complete, make up into a pillow hanging as follows. Trim the embroidery ten rows beyond the design. Cut a piece of iron-on interfacing to the same size and press on to the wrong side of the embroidery.

4 To create a hanging loop, cut a 25.5cm (10in) length of decorative cord and place the ends 2cm (¾in) from either side of embroidery, matching raw edges with the top edge of the trimmed embroidery. Cut the backing fabric to the same size as the trimmed embroidery and pin in place, right sides facing. Using matching sewing thread, stitch a 1.25cm (½in) seam all around, leaving an opening for turning at the bottom edge. Turn through to the right side and stuff with polyester filling.

5 Attach the remainder of the decorative cord by slipstitching it around all edges, beginning at centre bottom. Tuck the cord into the gap and slipstitch closed. To finish off, attach a decorative button at the centre bottom.

Heart Strings

DMC stranded cotton

Cross stitch

■ 208	□ 775	□ 3348
V 209	■ 797	■ 3687
■ 210	⊙ 798	╱ 3688
■ 310	■ 799	□ 3689
− 676	╱ 869	⋏ 3756
□ 677	■ 945	■ 3829
□ 726	□ 951	╲ 3840
O 727	■ 3346	• blanc
✕ 729	I 3347	

French knots

● 208
● 310
○ 726
● 797
● 3346
● 3687
○ blanc

Backstitch

— 208
— 310
— 797
— 3346

Native American Wisdom

In Native American culture, each nation has made use of dream catchers to protect their people as they slept. Their ring-shaped form represents the sacred circle and the woven sinew and beads tell of the spiritual web of life. Placed close to the sleeping spot, it is believed that bad dreams will be caught in the centre of the web and in the morning light they will evaporate like the dew. The good dreams are caught on the fragile feathers and trickle down through the night providing tranquillity and peace for the protected sleeper.

In soft blues, violets and earthy shades of brown, these feathered talismans keep watch on the night sky, holding our dreams in safe keeping and releasing the promise of the future into our hands.

Native American Wisdom Sampler

Stitch count
212h x 156w

Design size
38.5 x 28.5cm (15 x 11in)

Materials

51 x 40.5cm (20 x 16in) antique white 14-count Aida

DMC stranded cotton (floss) as listed in chart key

Tapestry needle size 24

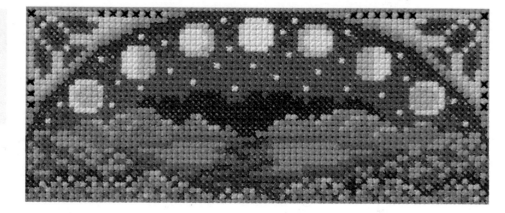

1 Prepare for work, referring to Techniques if necessary. Find and mark the centre of the fabric and circle the centre of the chart with a pen. This is a large design so use an embroidery frame if you wish.

2 Start stitching from the centre of the chart and fabric, using two strands of stranded cotton (floss) for cross stitches. Following the chart for colour changes, work all French knots using two strands wrapped once around the needle. Work the feather spines on the smallest feathers in backstitch with one strand and the body of all the feathers using long stitches and two strands, changing colours as on the chart. Work all other backstitches using one strand.

3 Once all stitching is complete, checked for missed stitches and then finish your picture by mounting and framing (see page 101).

Native American Wisdom

DMC stranded cotton

Cross stitch

◤ 208	■ 333	■ 470	676	✔ 799	3747
● 310	■ 355	471	╱ 677	╲ 806	◉ 3803
317	367	✚ 472	729	✕ 869	3829
318	◎ 368	597	━ 797	■ 898	• blanc
╱ 319	┐ 415	598	∣ 798	━ 992	

Backstitch/Long stitch

— 310	— 799
— 333	— 869
— 729	— 898
— 797	— 3829
— 798	

Cross stitch

Native
American
Wisdom

DMC
stranded
cotton

╲	208		333		470		676	V	799		3747
•	310		355		471	╱	677	╲	806	◉	3803
	317		367	+	472		729	×	869		3829
	318	○	368		597	−	797		898	•	blanc
╱	319	⌐	415		598	I	798	−	992		

Backstitch/Long stitch

—	310	—	799
—	333	—	869
—	729	—	898
—	797	—	3829
—	798		

Charted Alphabets

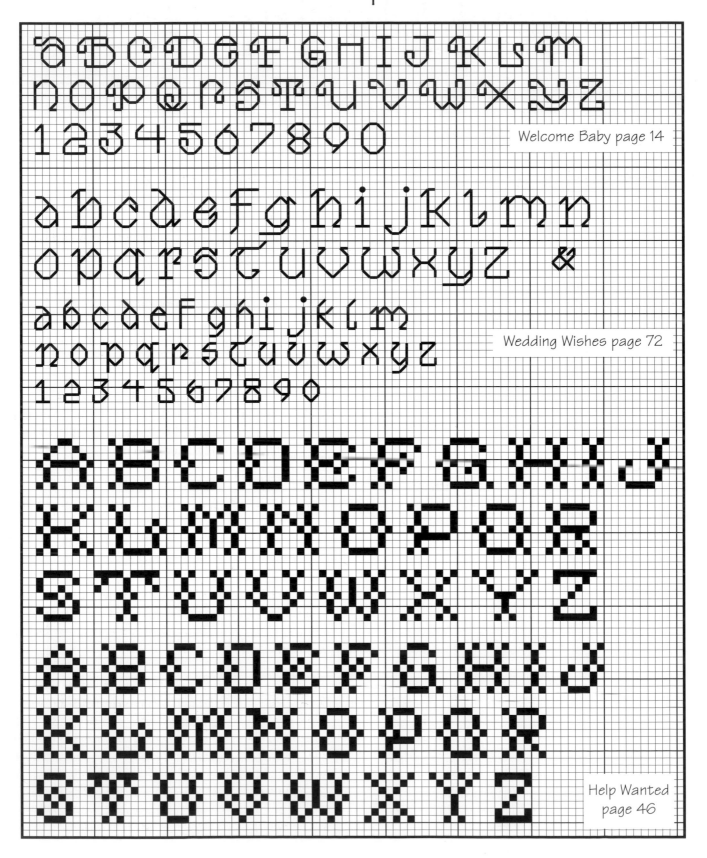

ABCDEFGHIJKLM
NOPQRSTUVWXYZ
1234567890

Welcome Baby page 14

abcdefghijklmn
opqrstuvwxyz &

abcdefghijklm
nopqrstuvwxyz
1234567890

Wedding Wishes page 72

ABCDEFGHIJ
KLMNOPQR
STUVWXYZ

ABCDEFGHIJ
KLMNOPQR
STUVWXYZ

Help Wanted
page 46

Materials, Techniques and Making Up

This section describes the materials and equipment required, the basic techniques used and the stitches needed to work the projects in the book. Specific making up methods are covered in the projects, with making up cards and framing pictures described on page 101. Refer to Suppliers on page 103 for useful addresses.

Materials

Very few materials are required for cross stitch.

Fabrics

The designs have been worked predominantly on a blockweave fabric called Aida. They could also be stitched on an evenweave such as linen but will need to be worked over two fabric threads instead of one block. If you change the gauge (count) of the material, that is the number of holes per inch, then the size of the finished work will alter accordingly (see Calculating Design Size, below).

Threads

The projects have been stitched with DMC stranded embroidery cotton (floss) but you could match the colours to other thread ranges (see DMC/Anchor conversion table on page 102). The six-stranded skeins can easily be split into separate threads. The project instructions tell you how many strands to use.

Needles

Tapestry needles, available in different sizes, are used for cross stitch as they have a rounded point and do not snag fabric. A thinner, beading needle will be needed to attach seed beads.

Frames

Whether you use an embroidery frame to keep your fabric taut while stitching is a matter of personal preference. Generally speaking, working with a frame helps to keep the tension even and prevent distortion, while working without a frame is faster and less cumbersome. There are various types on the market – look in your local needlework shop.

Techniques

Cross stitch embroidery requires few complicated techniques but your stitching will look its best if you follow the simple guidelines below.

Preparing the Fabric

Before starting, check the design size given with each project and make sure that this tallies with the size that you require for your finished embroidery. Your fabric should be at least 5cm (2in) larger all the way round than the finished size of the stitching, to allow for making up. Before beginning to stitch, neaten the edges of the fabric either by hemming or zigzag stitching to stop the fabric fraying as you work.

Finding the Fabric Centre

Regardless of which direction you work the design from it is important to find the centre point of the fabric in order to stitch the work centrally on the fabric. To find the centre, fold the fabric in half horizontally and then vertically, then tack (baste) along the folds (or mark with tailor's chalk). The centre point is where the two lines meet. This point on the fabric should correspond to the centre point on the chart. Remove any tacking (basting) on completion of the work.

Calculating Design Size

Each project gives the stitch count and finished design size but if you want to work the design on a different count fabric you will need to re-calculate the finished size. Divide the number of stitches in the design by the fabric count number, e.g., 140 stitches x 140 stitches ÷ 14-count = a design size of 10 x 10in (2.5 x 2.5cm). Working on evenweave usually means working over two threads, so divide the fabric count by two before you start.

Using Charts and Keys

The charts in this book are easy to work from. Each square on the chart represents one stitch. Each coloured square, or coloured square with a symbol, represents a thread colour, with the code number in the chart key. Some of the designs use fractional stitches (three-quarter cross stitches) to give more definition to the design and these are shown as a triangle within a square. Solid coloured lines show where backstitches or long stitches are to be worked. French knots are shown by coloured circles. Larger coloured circles with a dot indicate beads.

Each chart has arrows at the sides to show the centre point, which you could mark with a pen. Where charts have been split over several pages, the key is repeated. For your own use, you could colour photocopy and enlarge the charts and tape the parts together.

Starting and Finishing Stitching

Avoid using knots when starting and finishing as this will make your work lumpy when mounted. Instead, bring the needle up at the start of the first stitch, leaving a 'tail' of about 2.5cm (1in) at the back. Secure the tail by working the first few stitches over it. Start new threads by first passing the needle through several stitches on the back of the work.

To finish off thread, pass the needle through some nearby stitches on the wrong side of the work, then cut the thread off close to the fabric

The Stitches

Backstitch

Backstitches are used to give definition to a design and to outline areas. Many of the charts use different coloured backstitches. Follow Fig 1, bringing the needle up at 1 and down at 2, up at 3, down at 4 and so on.

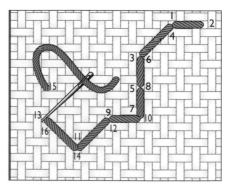

Fig 1 Backstitch

Cross Stitch

A cross stitch can be worked singly or in rows – a number of half cross stitches can be sewn in a line and completed on the return journey.

To make a cross stitch over one block of Aida, bring the needle up through the fabric at the bottom left side of the stitch (number 1 on Fig 2a) and cross diagonally to the top right corner (2). Push the needle through the hole and bring up through the bottom right corner (3), crossing the fabric diagonally to the top left corner to finish the stitch (4). To work the next stitch, push the needle up through the bottom left corner of the first stitch and repeat the steps above.

To work cross stitches in rows, stitch the first part of the stitch as above and repeat these half cross stitches along the row. Complete the crosses on the way back. Note: for neat stitching always finish the cross stitch with the top stitches facing the same diagonal direction.

Fig 2a Working a single cross stitch

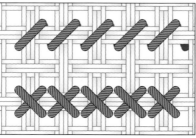

Fig 2b Working cross stitch in rows

French Knot

French knots have been used as eye highlights and details in some of the designs, in various colours. To work, follow Fig 3, bringing the needle and thread up through the fabric at the exact place where the knot is to be positioned. Wrap the thread once or twice around the needle (according to the project instructions), holding the thread firmly close to the needle, then twist the needle back through the fabric as close as possible to where it first emerged. Holding the knot down carefully, pull the thread through to the back leaving the knot on the surface, securing it with one small stitch on the back.

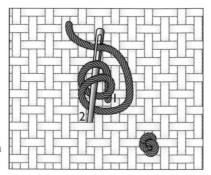

Fig 3 French knot

Long Stitch

This is used for feathers in the Native American Wisdom sampler. Simply work a long, straight stitch, starting and finishing at the points indicated on the chart.

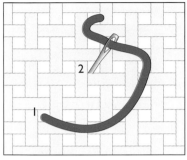

Fig 4 Long stitch

Three-quarter Cross Stitch

Three-quarter cross stitches give more detail and 'curves' to a design. These are shown on the charts as a triangle (half square). If working on evenweave, work the first half of a cross stitch as usual. Work the second 'quarter' over the top and down into the central hole to anchor the first half of the stitch. If working on Aida, push the needle through the centre block of the fabric.

Fig 5 Three-quarter cross stitch

Where two three-quarter stitches lie back to back in the space of one full cross stitch, work both of the respective quarter stitches into the central hole.

Attaching Beads

Adding beads will bring sparkle and texture to a cross stitch design. Attach seed beads using ordinary sewing thread that matches the fabric colour and a beading needle or very fine 'sharp' needle and a half or whole cross stitch.

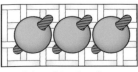

Fig 6 Attaching beads

Making up Your Work

The embroideries in this book are very versatile and can be made up in many ways. Generally, making up is included with each project but two general techniques are described here.

Making Up into a Card

Many of the designs or parts of the larger designs can be stitched and made up into cards. You will need: a ready-made card mount (aperture to fit the embroidery) and craft glue or double-sided tape.

Trim the edges of the embroidery to fit the card. Apply a thin coat of glue or a piece of double-sided tape to the inside of the card opening. Position the embroidery, checking that the stitching is central, and press down firmly. Fold the spare flap inside, sticking in place with glue or tape, and leave to dry before closing.

You can easily add a personal touch to ready-made card mounts by decorating them, gluing on ribbons, bows, beads, buttons, stickers and even personal drawings in waterproof markers. Visit your local stationery or craft store and explore all the possibilities.

Making Up as a Framed Picture

The designs make wonderful framed pictures. You will need: a picture frame (aperture to fit embroidery); a piece of plywood or heavyweight card slightly smaller than the frame; and adhesive tape or a staple gun.

Iron your embroidery and trim the edges, then centre it on the plywood or thick card. Fold the edges of the embroidery to the back and use adhesive tape or a staple gun to fix in place. Insert the picture into the frame and secure with adhesive tape or staples. For a more polished finish, with a wider choice of mounts and frames, take your work to a professional framer.

DMC/Anchor Thread Conversions

This DMC/Anchor conversion chart should only be used as a guide since exact comparisons cannot always be made. An asterisk * indicates that an Anchor shade has been used more than once so take great care to avoid duplication within a design.

DMC	Anchor	DMC	Anchor	DMC	Anchor	DMC	Anchor	DMC	Anchor	DMC	Anchor	DMC	Anchor	DMC	Anchor
B 5200	1	355	1014	604	55	781	308*	912	209	3023	899	3765	170	3846	1090
White	2	356	1013*	605	1094	782	308*	913	204	3024	388*	3766	167	3847	1076*
Ecru	387*	367	216	606	334	783	307	915	1029	3031	905*	3768	779	3848	1074*
150	59	368	214	608	330*	791	178	917	89	3032	898*	3770	1009	3849	1070*
151	73	369	1043	610	889	792	941	918	341	3033	387*	3772	1007	3850	188*
152	969	370	888*	611	898*	793	176*	919	340	3041	871	3773	1008	3851	186*
153	95*	371	887*	612	832	794	175	920	1004	3042	870	3774	778	3852	306*
154	873	372	887*	613	831	796	133	921	1003*	3045	888*	3776	1048*	3853	1003*
155	1030*	400	351	632	936	797	132	922	1003*	3046	887*	3777	1015	3854	313
156	118*	402	1047*	640	393	798	146	924	851	3047	887	3778	1013*	3855	311*
157	120*	407	914	642	392	799	145	926	850	3051	845*	3779	868	3856	347
158	178	413	236*	644	391	800	144	927	849	3052	844	3781	1050	3857	936*
159	120*	414	235*	645	273	801	359	928	274	3053	843	3782	388*	3858	1007
160	175*	415	398	646	8581*	806	169	930	1035	3064	883	3787	904*	3859	914*
161	176	420	374	647	1040	807	168	931	1034	3072	397	3790	904*	3860	379*
162	159*	422	372	648	900	809	130	932	1033	3078	292	3799	236*	3861	378
163	877	433	358	666	46	813	161*	934	852*	3325	129	3801	1098	3862	358*
164	240*	434	310	676	891	814	45	935	861	3326	36	3802	1019*	3863	379*
165	278*	435	365	677	361*	815	44	936	846	3328	1024	3803	69	3864	376
166	280*	436	363	680	901*	816	43	937	268*	3340	329	3804	63*	3865	2*
167	375*	437	362	699	923*	817	13*	938	381	3341	328	3805	62*	3866	926*
168	274*	444	291	700	228	818	23*	939	152*	3345	268*	3806	62*	48	1207
169	849*	445	288	701	227	819	271	943	189	3346	267*	3807	122	51	1220*
208	110	451	233	702	226	820	134	945	881	3347	266*	3808	1068	52	1209*
209	109	452	232	703	238	822	390	946	332	3348	264	3809	1066*	57	1203*
210	108	453	231	704	256*	823	152*	947	330*	3350	77	3810	1066*	61	1218*
211	342	469	267*	712	926	824	164	948	1011	3354	74	3811	1060	62	1202*
221	897*	470	266*	718	88	825	162*	950	4146	3362	263	3812	188	67	1212
223	895	471	265	720	326	826	161*	951	1010	3363	262	3813	875*	69	1218*
224	895	472	253	721	324	827	160	954	203*	3364	261	3814	1074	75	1206*
225	1026	498	1005	722	323*	828	9159	955	203*	3371	382	3815	877*	90	1217*
300	352	500	683	725	305*	829	906	956	40*	3607	87	3816	876*	91	1211
301	1049*	501	878	726	295*	830	277*	957	50	3608	86	3817	875*	92	1215*
304	19	502	877*	727	293	831	277*	958	187	3609	85	3818	923*	93	1210*
307	289	503	876*	729	890	832	907*	959	186	3685	1028	3819	278	94	1216
309	42	504	206*	730	845*	833	874*	961	76*	3687	68	3820	306	95	1209*
310	403	517	162*	731	281*	834	874*	962	75*	3688	75*	3821	305*	99	1204
311	148	518	1039	732	281*	838	1088	963	23*	3689	49	3822	295*	101	1213*
312	979	519	1038	733	280	839	1086	964	185	3705	35*	3823	386	102	1209*
315	1019*	520	862*	734	279	840	1084	966	240	3706	33*	3824	8*	103	1210*
316	1017	522	860	738	361*	841	1082	970	925	3708	31	3825	323*	104	1217*
317	400	523	859	739	366	842	1080	971	316*	3712	1023	3826	1049*	105	1218*
318	235*	524	858	740	316*	844	1041	972	298	3713	1020	3827	311	106	1203*
319	1044*	535	401	741	304	869	375	973	290	3716	25	3828	373	107	1203*
320	215	543	933	742	303	890	218	975	357	3721	896	3829	901*	108	1220*
321	47	550	101*	743	302	891	35*	976	1001	3722	1027	3830	5975	111	1218*
322	978	552	99	744	301	892	33*	977	1002	3726	1018	3831	29	112	1201*
326	59*	553	98	745	300	893	27	986	246	3727	1016	3832	28	113	1210*
327	101*	554	95	746	275	894	26	987	244	3731	76*	3833	31*	114	1213*
333	119	561	212	747	158	895	1044*	988	243	3733	75*	3834	100*	115	1206*
334	977	562	210	754	1012	898	380	989	242	3740	872	3835	98*	121	1210*
335	40*	563	208	758	9575	899	38	991	1076	3743	869	3836	90	122	1215*
336	150	564	206*	760	1022	900	333	992	1072	3746	1030	3837	100*	124	1210*
340	118	580	924	761	1021	902	897*	993	1070	3747	120	3838	177	125	1213*
341	117*	581	281*	762	234	904	258	995	410	3750	1036	3839	176*	126	1209*
347	1025	597	1064	772	259*	905	257	996	433	3752	1032	3840	120*		
349	13*	598	1062	775	128	906	256*	3011	856	3753	1031	3841	159*		
350	11	600	59*	776	24	907	255	3012	855	3755	140	3842	164*		
351	10	601	63*	778	968	909	923*	3013	853	3756	1037	3843	1089*		
352	9	602	57	779	380*	910	230	3021	905*	3760	162*	3844	410*		
353	8*	603	62*	780	309	911	205	3022	8581*	3761	928	3845	1089*		

Suppliers

Charles Craft Inc
PO Box 1049,
Laurenburg, NC 28353, USA
tel: 910 844 3521
email: ccraft@carolina.net
website: www.charlescraft.com
Cross stitch fabrics and many useful pre-finished items

Coats Crafts UK
PO Box 22, Lingfield Estate,
McMullen Road, Darlington,
County Durham DL1 1YQ, UK
tel: 01325 365457 (for a list of stockists)
For Anchor stranded cotton (floss) and other embroidery supplies (Coats also supply some Charles Craft products)

Design Works Crafts Inc
170 Wilbur Place, Bohemia,
NY 11716, USA
tel: 631 244 5749
fax: 631 244 6138
email: customerservice@
designworkscrafts.com
For Joan Elliott cross stitch kits and for card mounts

DMC Creative World
Pullman Road, Wigston,
Leicestershire LE18 2DY, UK
tel: 0116 281 1040
fax: 0116 281 3592
website: www.dmc/cw.com
For stranded cotton (floss) and many other embroidery supplies

Framecraft Miniatures Ltd
372–376 Summer Lane,
Hockley, Birmingham
B19 3QA, UK
tel: 0121 212 0551
fax: 0121 212 0552
website: www.framecraft.com
For trinket bowls and boxes, notebook covers, pincushions, and many other items with cross stitch inserts

Gay Bowles Sales Inc
PO Box 1060, Janesville,
WI 53547, USA
tel: 608 754 9466
fax: 608 754 0665
email millhill@inwave.com
website: www.millhill.com
For Mill Hill beads and for Framecraft products

Kreinik Manufacturing Company Inc
3106 Timanus Lane,
Suite 101, Baltimore,
MD 21244, USA
tel: 1800 537 2166
email: kreinik@kreinik.com
website: www.kreinik.com
For a wide range of metallic threads

Market Square Ltd
Wing Farm, Longbridge
Deverill,Warminster,
Wiltshire BA12 7DD, UK
tel: 01985 841041
fax: 01985 541042
For embroidery work boxes and trinket boxes

The WARM Company
954 East Union Street,
Seattle, WA 98122, USA
tel: 1 800 234 WARM
website: www.warmcompany.com
UK Distributor:
W. Williams & Sons Ltd,
Regent House, 1 Thane Villas,
London N7 7PH, UK
tel: 0207 2637311
fax: 0207 2814760
website: www.wwilliams.co.uk
For polyester filling, cotton wadding (batting) and Steam-A-Seam 2 fusible web

Zweigart/Joan Toggit Ltd
262 Old New Brunswick Road,
Suite E, Piscataway,
NJ 08854-3756, USA
tel: 732 562 8888
email: info@zweigart.com
website: www.zweigart.com
For cross stitch fabrics and pre-finished table linens

Acknowledgments

Words fall short of expressing the gratitude I feel towards all the wonderful stitchers that I have come to know while working on this book: Bev Ritter, Rindy Richards, Judy Trochimiak, Lori West, Meem Breyer, Linda Steffen, Helen McClain, Donna Snyder, Belinda Barnhart, Linda Moss, Regina Kimbrell, Judy Suleski and Lisa Rabon – thank you all for your wonderful talents, keen eyes and supportive words while bringing my designs to fruition.

With heartfelt appreciation I want to thank everyone at David & Charles whose efforts have made this book possible. To Ali Myer and Lisa Forrester for their wonderful layout and design and to Lucy Mason for her lovely photography. I am especially grateful to Sandra Pruski, not only for her incredible ability to keep track of everything involved in putting this all together but also for her friendship and support. To Cheryl Brown, my thanks again for this delightful book proposal and for your ever-present encouragement and enthusiasm. The friendship and easy working relationship I have shared with my editor, Lin Clements, has truly been a gift. Thank you Lin.

It is a comfort to know that friends and family have been here not only to help me through the stress of deadlines, artist's block and all such matters, but also to share the many joys and pleasures of creating *Cross Stitch Sentiments & Sayings*. With love, I thank you all.

About the Author

Joan Elliott has been creating needlework designs for over thirty years, enchanting stitching enthusiasts the world over with her unique humour and charm. Design Works Crafts Inc in the United States (see Suppliers) produce kits of many of her designs and she remains their leading artist.

Her debut book for David & Charles, *A Cross Stitcher's Oriental Odyssey* was followed by the equally successful *Cross Stitch Teddies*. Her third book *Cross Stitch Sentiments & Sayings* has allowed her to combine her creativity as an artist with her love of language to create projects that will amuse, motivate and inspire all stitchers.

Joan divides her time between Brooklyn, New York and southern Vermont and feels blessed that she and her husband have the opportunity to enjoy and share the many joys and experiences that both city and country life have to offer.

Index

A
alphabets 98

B
baby
    card 16–17, 98
    sampler 14–15, 18–19, 98
backstitch 100
bathroom 21, 22–3, 25
beads 75, 99, 101
bookmark 54, 56–9
bowl lid 55, 57

C
cards
    baby 16–17, 98
    birthday 61, 62
    friendship 8–9, 60, 61, 62, 64–5
    garden sayings 42–3
    making up 101
    parents 61, 62–3
    pure indulgence 78, 81, 85
    sweet sentiments 60–5
    teddy bears 46–51
    Wisdom of the East 53, 59
Celtic Spirit
    pincushion 30
    sachet 31
    sampler 28–9, 32–5
charts, using 100
coaster, friendship 8–9
cook, sampler 21, 22, 24
cross stitch 100

D
dieting 78–85
dream catchers 93–7

F
fabrics 99
frames, embroidery 99
French knot 100
fridge magnets 78, 80, 85
friendship
    cards 8–9, 60, 61, 62, 64–5
    coaster 8–9
    sampler 6–7, 10–13, 28

G
garden
    cards 42–3
    plant pokes 42–3
    sampler 40–1, 44–5

H
hangings see samplers
home 20–7, 36–9, 46
housework 21, 22–3, 25–7, 46–51, 98

K
kind deeds 86–8, 90
knots 100

L
long stitch 101
love, pillow 87, 89, 91

M
making up 101
materials 99

N
Native American wisdom, sampler 93–7
needles 99
notices see samplers

P
parents, cards 61, 62–3
pictures, making up 101
pillow
    love saying 87, 89, 91
    wedding ring 72, 74–5, 98
pincushion 30
pokes, plant 42–3
pure indulgence
    cards 78, 81, 85
    fridge magnets 78, 80, 85
    notices 78–9, 82–4

S
sachets 31, 55, 58–9
samplers
    baby 14–15, 18–19, 98
    bathroom 21, 22–3, 25
    Celtic Spirit 28–9, 32–5
    cook 21, 22, 24
    friendship 6–7, 10–13, 28
    garden 40–1, 44–5
    help wanted 46–51, 98
    history 4
    home 36–9, 46
    housework 21, 22–3, 25–7
    love/kind deeds 86–91
    Native American wisdom 93–7
    pure indulgence 78–80, 82–4
    wedding 72–3, 75–7, 98
    Wisdom of the East 52–4, 56–9
    work 66–71
size of project 99
stitches 100–1
suppliers 103

T
techniques 99–100
teddy bears
    cards 46–51, 61, 63, 65
    help wanted 46–51, 98
    hug hanging 86, 88, 90
    sampler 36–9
    welcome baby 14–19
thread 99, 102
three-quarter cross stitch 101

W
wedding
    ring pillow 72, 74–5, 98
    sampler 72–3, 75–7, 98
Wisdom of the East
    bookmark 54, 56–9
    bowl lid 55, 57
    card 53, 59
    sachet 55, 58–9
    sampler 52–4, 56–9
work, samplers 66–71